Becoming

A

Better You

Scripture quotations, unless otherwise noted, are from the New
International Version of the Bible.

ISBN-13: 978-0692102053
ISBN-10: 0692102051

Lighted Paths Publishing
Printed in the United States of America

Becoming

A

Better You

Embracing "a better self" along
life's journey through spiritual awakening,
change, and the power of God's Love

Chavelle Dallas

Dedications

This book is dedicated first and foremost to the glory of God. I love You and I thank You! I offer this book up to You as the first fruit of my inspirational labor. I pray it is pleasing and acceptable in your sight. xoxo

To my sons, my parents, my family, special loved ones, and all my wonderful friends - you all help to inspire and encourage me through every single thing in life. I want to say thank you, thank you, and thank you! I love you and appreciate you all!

Chavelle Dallas

Contents

Chapter 1 – The Breakdown

Chapter 2 – The Buildup

The Breakdown

Introduction

I Am a Better Me

I don't want to be perfect! No, I really don't. And I don't strive to be. But each day I find myself making a conscious effort to become a better version of myself. A peaceful, calm, strong, balanced, happy, and relaxed version of myself! A person who graciously loves herself unconditionally! A person who has justly accepted her insecurities, her flaws and her mistakes in life, yet still sees her soul as being quite beautiful. A person who has courageously fought to overcome many of life's potholes and many life challenges, and is still here to talk about them and say that all is ok, and all is well within her soul.

I'm admiring a person who awake in the mornings wholeheartedly giving God thanks for each new day. I have fallen in love with this person who frequently seeks and depend on God for wisdom, power, and the strength to deal with and subdue any negativity that comes her way. I respect and honor this person who takes on challenges of any new struggle and have them work out for a greater good in her life. And lastly, I uphold this person who does not want to spend another day without the love, the joy, the peace, and the blessings of God evident in her daily life! Yes, I am now this person and this person is me!

To God be the glory for all I've experienced in life. I thank Him for the good, the bad, the ups, and the downs. I thank Him for the love, the pain, the failures, and the successes. For all of that has brought me right here. And here for me is a place of great love, great understanding, great peace, and great compassion. I am a personal witness and I give my full testimony to the truth that in a world filled with so much hurt, hate, pain, disappointment, failure and destruction, we can still have love, we can still have peace, and we can still have hope! No, I'm not interested in being perfect. Not even a little bit! But every day I make a conscious decision, backed by effort, to become A Better Me. Welcome to "Becoming a Better You." There is no limit to what we can achieve internally!

2. Life

Life! It is definitely not easy! It's not easy and it hardly ever pans out exactly the way we plan or imagine it will! There are often many obstacles to face, many hills to climb, and many stumbling blocks in our path. And though we may conquer many of those adverse situations, most of us still seemingly have a sense of not truly understanding where and how we fit into this place we call life. Somehow, life still leaves us confused and frustrated. Life leaves us searching for answers and looking for directions. Life leaves us uncertain, unsettled, and just plain tired of being tired.

If life never dealt us any problems or gave us anything uncomfortable to ever have to cope with and overcome, our living would truly be grand! Unfortunately, that is not the reality of the world we live in. And as long as we are living in this world, there will always be something that has to be dealt with. Some things may not scream out as loud as others. And some things may not cause much chaos in our lives. But they are all potential problems designed to harden our hearts, burden our souls, and attempt to keep us from experiencing true joy and peace.

However, people who are serious about becoming a better person must acknowledge and accept that the true successors in life will never get the prize without the pain. It is the pain of the struggle, the pain of the hard work, the pain of the sacrifices, and the pain of the fight. It is the pain of the heartaches, the pain of the consequences, the pain of the humility, and the pain of the defeats. It is the pain of the tears, the pain of the compromises, and the pain of the dedication. And most importantly, it is the pain of surrendering, the pain of forgiving, and the pain of the courage it takes to keep getting back up and persevering after life has continuously knocked us down. When put into proper perspective, these pains can help us find ourselves and may give us most of the answers we seek in life. These pains can steer us into a place of growth, maturity, and fulfillment. These pains can condition us into becoming better people.

As we travel along life's journey, it will benefit us to look at life as a big book of education. A book that's readily available for us to continuously learn from. Let's not view life as being a goal we should strive to live as "complete." When I think of the word complete, I think of things being finished, ended, or having no parts missing. With that in mind, we should never strive for completeness in life on the level of being totally finished or ended. Especially because we continuously "live out" our lives here on earth! There's nothing wrong with striving for a peaceful, balanced, and well maintained (wholesome) life, but "a complete life" well that may add a little bit of arrogance to one's thoughts and character.

I believe it is difficult for people who consider their lives to be complete to hear the cries and concerns of others. It's hard for them to hear the broken hearts of the world and see others broken lives. I also believe that people who categorize their lives as complete mainly focus on all things inside of their own seemingly perfect and complete worlds. Therefore, I choose not to view, teach, speak on, or embrace life as something we should strive to live as complete. To continuously grow and challenge ourselves will always be a catalyst for great change. And a big part of our great change will come once we begin to take proper steps to get involved with our own lives.

Constructive steps will continuously lead us into a place of growth and maturity. With growth and maturity, we begin to really take charge of the things we can control. We begin to diligently seek the necessary tools to start co-creating the life we desire to live. This is why it is imperative that we become involved with our own lives. It's important because although God gives us the wisdom and tools to live life and become better people, He will not take the action steps for us. Nor will He make every little decision for us. We have to gather up the strength and the courage to take action steps for ourselves. We need the bravery and confidence to trust ourselves with the wisdom and knowledge we will receive when we are seeking to get better, to be better, and to do better.

True, it is not easy to live this life! But living it is exactly what we must do. Life's uncertainties will surely hit us with big blows every now and then, but it doesn't have to be the end of our story. It doesn't have to deaden our souls! To productively navigate through life, we have to be authentic, vulnerable, teachable, and moldable. We must access our reality, accept life's challenges, and embrace opportunities that will help us learn how to make the best of our situations! Once we begin to master those skills, we will then be able to grasp a very real chance to be healed, whole, happy, and better people. We can grasp a real chance to really enjoy the goodness of life.

Becoming a better person does not keep the focus on our yesterdays. Becoming a better person will not be based upon our tomorrows. Becoming a better person should only focus on what we are willing to do inside each and every new and present day to become a better person. What steps are we willing to take? What decisions are we willing to make? What are we willing to learn? What are we willing to stand up for? How are we willing to grow? What are we willing to forgive, to let go, and to let be in order to enjoy a better life this day? These are just some of the questions we will have to regularly ask ourselves and be able to answer.

Note: There is wisdom, power, strength, and every good thing we need in our lives available to all of us. If we are willing to reach deep inside our hearts and grab those good things, we can live life more at ease. If there is one good and merciful side to having problems and learning how to navigate through life, it is definitely learning, knowing, and trusting that we have a friend in The Problem Solver and The Great Navigator. The "ONE" I am speaking of is none other than our sovereign God whom I know and have accepted through my Lord and Savior Jesus Christ. He is "THE" PROBLEM SOLVER, "THE" NAVIGATOR, and "THE" HIGHER POWER! He can be there in times of trouble when we allow Him to be! He is comfort for the comfortless, rest for the restless, peace for the non-peaceful, joy for the joyless, and so very much more. God is a perfectly good God and when we love on Him, trust in Him, and lean and depend on Him ... all things really do work together for our good.

Our lives include many miracles every single day! And through all we go through, we can still "be" grateful and thankful to God for something! Our reality won't always be a happy, comfortable, and peaceful place to dwell in. And we won't always "feel" grateful and thankful. But there is a difference between being and feeling. When we can "be" grateful and thankful, it doesn't matter how we feel. "Being" grateful and thankful acknowledges God's sovereignty just because we know and trust that He exists. It means we trust He's bigger than us, He knows more than we know, and He is available to help us through it all.

Life is not easy. But the ultimate truth about life is that it is ALL under God's control! And with our limited abilities, we need His love, His humbleness, His mercy, and His compassion. We need His forgiveness, His strength, His patience, and His understanding. We need His wisdom, His grace, His Being, and absolutely EVERYTHING about Him, to embrace life, love, and all paths to becoming better people.

3. Storms of Life

Why do we experience storms in our lives? Storms enter our lives for many different reasons. But all storms can be avenues to seeking God and maturing in heart, mind, and spirit. Storms of life help us to tap into the wisdom, strength, and power of God that lies dormant within us. Storms come to force us to accept change. Storms may come to shift us out of our comfort zones. Storms come to help us face our fears and our insecurities. Storms may come to help us deal with, clean up, and build up our inner selves. Storms come because of bad choices we have made in life. Storms may come to bring a halt to our own plans and make us aware of and acknowledge that there is a Mighty God who is the ultimate planner of life. And storms may also come to make us dig deep and wake up God's purpose for our lives.

These are not all the reasons why storms may enter into our lives, but exploring these will reveal truths that will help us get to the root of most things we experience in life. Let's deal with some of these reasons individually.

Storms Force Us to Accept Change

Without being forced, some of us will never change anything! We won't change our attitudes, our ways of thinking, our jobs, our priorities or anything. We repeat clichés like, "if it's not broke then don't fix it, this is just the way I am, or God knows my heart." These expressions will keep our minds trapped into our ways of thinking and doing things. They will also keep us immature and stagnant in life. Some of us will do anything to continuously keep our lives exactly the same, not realizing, where there is no change there is also no growth. And where there is no growth, things regress, wither, and possibly die.

Storms teach those of us who don't like change that change is inevitable. Change is the one thing we can always depend on to take place in our lives. Just like calendar seasons' change, so will the seasons of our lives! And if we aren't adaptable to the changes, we will wake up one morning and realize that life has somehow passed us by. God is the only entity who stays the same, and being that He is the I AM, He can be who He is, who He was, and whoever we need Him to be, ALL AT THE SAME TIME and in any given moment.

We can't become our better selves if we are refusing change. When we refuse change, we are subconsciously asking life to leave us behind, to isolate us, and to lock us into a specific place and time. When we refuse change, we are subconsciously telling our selves that growth does not matter, that love does not matter, and that evolving as a human being does not matter. When we refuse change, we are telling our loved ones that they don't matter enough! We are subconsciously telling them that we are not willing to mature and grow with them. And in an indirect way, we are also telling our loved ones that we are not willing to meet their needs anymore. I say that because when people are not on the same level and when people cannot get on the same page in life - emotional, mental, physical, and spiritual needs are going to go unmet.

In order to grow spiritually, mentally, and emotionally, we must be willing to accept and adapt to change. We must also be willing to make efforts to change. When striving to become a better person, we can't have most of our growth hindered because without proper growth in most areas in our lives, we act out as people in adult bodies but with the minds, actions, and reactions of small children or teenagers. (Scary isn't it)! It's scary to think of our lives in that manner, but it is true.

Also, some situations in our lives won't ever change until we have taken the initiative to change. We can be missing out on so many blessings for ourselves and our loved ones by not being open to productively changing who we are and how we look at life. Wouldn't it be disappointing to get to Heaven only to find out that we were supposed to be business owners, millionaires, or were supposed to play a major role in helping others, but we didn't receive those blessings, nor were we ever able to be a blessing to others "only" because we refused change? What if we got to Heaven and found out we had to settle for struggling and lack the majority of our lives here on earth "only" because we refused change? What if God showed us how our refusal to change affected our entire family in ways that were very negative and caused them to be self-destructive and make lots of very poor decisions?

Refusing change (learning and growing) can have major life-changing effects on ourselves as well as the people around us. It can also affect the generations who comes after us. In order to leave an honorable and respectable legacy behind, we have to become that honorable and respectable legacy! We have to become the change, the hope, and the inspiration that others may need to see. Embrace opportunities to change!

Storms Help Us to Deal With Our Inner self

How many times have we looked at others and pointed out their faults? How many times have we blamed others for all the wrong going on in our lives, or where we are in life? How many times have we judged someone and their situation only to end up in the same situation or worse?

Romans 2:1 reads: (NIV) *You, therefore, have no excuse, you who pass judgment on someone else, for at whatever point you judge another, you are condemning yourself, because you who pass judgement do the same things.*

To break that scripture down a little more, the scripture is telling us that the same things we are judgmental about in others are usually the same things that reside in our own lives. It's crazy how some of us can take on a condemning "I would never do that" attitude about something someone else is doing then somehow end up in the exact same situation as the person we judged. We are quick to judge others (to judge means to already form an opinion of or make a decision about), not realizing, we can and will bring that same condemnation (strong criticism, disapproval, punishment, judgement) down upon ourselves.

It's fairly easy to make judgements about others when we see ourselves as being better than someone else. We see ourselves as better than others when we aren't aware of our true selves and our own shortcomings. Just know that the moment we think we are better than others or are immune to specific temptations, is the moment we have begun to deceive ourselves. In that moment, we breathe life into setting ourselves up for disappointment and a major fall. Life will prove to every single one of us that we all fall short of being the super great people we might think we are!

Storms that help us deal with our inner selves teach us that we are no better than the next person. We are no better than anyone else, nor are we above any kind of temptation. Instead of judging others, we should thank God for His grace and His mercy and know that it is ONLY because of God, we are not in some of the same situations our fellow men and women get caught up in. We aren't aware of what lies inactive in our souls; therefore, these storms have a way of making us see our own weaknesses. These storms force us to put down the pointed finger, to not think so highly of ourselves, and to bridle this tongue of ours. Remember in Matthew 26: 33-35, when Jesus told Peter that he (Peter) would deny Him three times before the cock crowed? Peter insisted he would never deny Jesus and what happened? Peter did exactly what he thought and insisted he would never do.

We don't know the depth of all that is on the inside of us and what could come forward if put under the right kinds of stress, pressure, and desperation. We don't know what we would do if we were ever in survival mode. There are people in prison today who never thought they would ever kill anyone. There are alcoholics who thought they would never drink. Drug addicts who thought they would never do drugs; etc. It is so important to get to know ourselves. We need to know and accept that we are truly capable of performing ALL acts good, bad, saintly, or sinister. We must be fully aware of all sides of ourselves; the good, the bad, the ugly, and the indifferent. It's imperative that we take the steps and do the work to make those inner connections with all sides of self when striving to become a better person.

Storms that deal with and bring forth our inner selves are beneficial to our lives. But in order for them to be effective, we have to accept the truth of who we are; and accept the truth of the person that's being revealed to us. It's ok when different sides of our selves are revealed. It's ok because we all have different sides and sometimes the person we truly are is not the person we present to the outside world every day. That's sometimes okay too, but unless we have made those inner connections to truly know all sides of who we really are, it may seem as if we are unbalanced and are living double lives. To others we may seem out of balance, unstable, and inauthentic.

Without the connection, the life we show to others can easily become, or seem to be (to others), a fabrication of what we want others to think and believe about us. It becomes or depicts a fabrication of who we want to be, how we want to live, and how we want to feel on the inside. Fabricated lives are tiresome visages and a person will never truly be happy while living a fabricated life. Fabricated lives will make a person feel as if he/she is always "putting on" instead of being true to his/her authentic self. Making the connections to all sides of ourselves is "key" to our authenticity! We can feel okay about presenting different sides of who we are to people when all the sides are connected, balanced, and are being genuine and true to self. For example, if someone on the outside says that I'm mean and I can look at myself and say, "You know what, depending on the situation, I can be mean sometimes." Then I have made that connection and I am being genuine and true to self. Another example: if a lot of people are saying I'm mean and I say, "I'm not mean, they just don't understand me!" Or if I say, "I'm not mean; they are the ones with the problem!" In those examples, it's obvious that I may be in denial and am not being true or genuine to self. We should never accept and be true to a lie that people may say about us. But we should explore why they are saying it and try to make the connection with "the why." If the statement is 100% not true, we must stand in our truth and be genuine and true to self. If the statement keeps coming around and may or may not have a little truth to it, we should explore it and allow the understanding and connection with "the why" keep us genuine and true to self!

Note: We've got to know who we were, who we portray, and open to how others perceive us, in order to know and understand all of who we really are. We have to know where we have been to understand where we are presently. That helps us to make some productive decisions as to where we are trying to go in life. Don't be afraid to face, accept, and deal with all that may lie within us. We can't be afraid to be totally honest with our selves.

Bad Choices We Made in Life

Galatians 6: 7-8 reads: *Be not deceived; God is not mocked: For whatsoever a man soweth, that shall he also reap. For he that soweth to his flesh shall of the flesh reap corruption; but he that soweth to the spirit shall of the spirit reap life everlasting.*

God's spiritual laws and principles apply to all of us. God has laws and principles set in place for a reason and everyone will be accountable to them rather we choose to believe in Him or not. There are spiritual laws as well as laws of the land in place. Every human will have to fall under subjection to and be judged and chastised by them according to God and life. To break God's spiritual laws and not heed to His principles, or to break laws of life and governing authorities and not have to suffer the consequences and discipline for any of them, would be to escape them. To escape them would be making a mockery out of God and God will not be mocked!

Hebrews 12:5-11 (NIV) reads: *And have you completely forgotten this word of encouragement that addresses you as a father addresses his son (or daughter)? It says, "My son (daughter), do not make light of the Lord's discipline, and do not lose heart (give up) when He rebukes (scold, reprimand, admonish) you, because the Lord disciplines the one He loves and He chastens (humbles) everyone He accepts as His son (daughter). Endure hardship as discipline; God is treating you as His children. For what children are not disciplined by their father? If you are not disciplined (and everyone is disciplined), then you are not legitimate, not true sons and daughters at all. Moreover, we have all had human fathers who disciplined us and we respected them for it. How much more should we submit to the Father of spirit and live! They disciplined us for a little while as they thought best; but God disciplines us for our good, in order that we may share in His holiness. No discipline seems pleasant at the time, but painful. Later on, however, it produces a harvest of righteousness and peace for those who have been trained (received experience) by it.*

God knows discipline for lack of awareness and lack of spiritual awareness to His laws, principles, and the bad choices we have made in life, will be grievous (dreadful) and not enjoyable. But if we can endure this awful time, the result of the discipline will bring us peace and we will slowly begin our journey to become better people. As we learn to adhere to God's golden rules, our lives will begin to change for the better. As God's children, there must be discipline in our lives! And though God disciplines us, He is no different from a loving parent who disciplines his or her child/children. He does it because He loves us. He does it to help guide us into something new and something better.

Where we are in life today is a manifestation, as well as an indication, of the choices we have made in the past. Where we will be in life in the future, will be a manifestation, as well as an indication, of the choices we will make each new day leading into our futures. God allows us to make choices on how we want to live out our lives. We need to be keenly aware of the choices we make and the possible consequences of each choice. We need to know that our choices, both good and bad, will play out their entire roles in our lives.

Note: Whatever places we may find ourselves in life as we come into clearer understandings of the choices we have made, we should talk to God about it. We need to give a voice to those exact places! Just open our mouths and let out all of our truths and emotions no matter what we are feeling! We can feel free to talk to God just as if we were talking to our very best friend. He is there to hear it all! If we need forgiveness, we can repent and ask God for forgiveness. If we need to express anger, we can do that too. God is big enough to take our angry outbursts! He is big enough to handle all that we feel we need to express and whatever we want to express to Him.

Storms Build Inner Strength

Inner strength serves multiple purposes in our lives. Inner strength gives us power to control emotions and feelings in a respectable way. It gives us courage to stand up for what is right and for all that is good in our lives and for our lives. Inner strength helps us to find our voice and not allow anything or anyone to silence it. Inner strength also gives us the power to change our situations and our lives for the better!

We build inner strength when we begin to STOP reacting to life, to people, and to situations. Reacting means to conduct ourselves or behave in a particular way in response to something. It also means to act in opposition or with hostility to a force or influence. Instead of reacting, inner strength allows us to respond. Respond means to say something in reply or in return. The effectiveness responding gives us that reacting does not give us is "a thought out choice, action, answer, or reply." Responding allows us to think about what we should do and say before we actually do and say anything, whereas reacting is associated with being a bit harsh and immediate. Reacting is more of a "you did or said this to me, so I am doing or saying this to you" type of behavior. Though it is sometimes difficult to be respectable and peaceful (exemplify inner strength) in the midst of some types of adversity, the more we practice responding instead of reacting, the better we will become at it.

Inner strength also helps us to build character. Having character makes it easier for us to stand behind all we say and do. Without character to add value, trust, and promise to who and what we portray in life, we are only people making noise! Inner strength helps us to not be noise makers. It helps us to be people who are honest, accountable, and aware of our dealings in life. It builds integrity and integrity alone will bring all sorts of blessings and favor our way. Integrity will also help open doors of opportunity in our lives because when people know and feel that we are people who can be trusted to do exactly or beyond what we say we are going to do, they will be more apt to associate themselves with us. And once we become trusted associates, people may possibly make room for us to be a blessing to them and others in some way.

Note: Storms may come, but like all storms they eventually pass. They may cause a mess while they are present in our lives, but our lives are restorable. We may have to rebuild, adjust to new ways of doing things, or totally change directions in life, but life can be blessed, joyous, and fulfilling in light of the storms we may go through. Wherever our storms lead us in life, it can all be ok. It can be ok if we trust and know that wherever we end up, God will be there also.

4. Unresolved Matters

Along our journey to become a better person, we must confront and bring to closure unresolved matters in our lives. Unresolved matters consist of people and situations that have caused, or are causing, us any type of grief, sorrow, anger, despair, or discomfort. Matters are unresolved if there has not been a definite end (closure) to it, or if we don't have any peace about it. Matters are unresolved if they keep us stuck in life and prevents us from prospering or moving forward. If there are feelings and emotions attached to matters that make us feel vexed or any type of hate, blame, resentment, fear, guilt, vengeance, chaos, anger, or any sort of ill-will, the matter is unresolved.

Every accomplished goal, dream, or desire is achieved by building it upon some type of foundation. The key to making our goals, dreams, and desires a lasting and fulfilling reality will largely be based upon the strength, the contents, and the character of the foundation it is built upon. It is the same scenario when we are striving to become a better person. It is at this point where unresolved matters will play a vital role in our lives. They are vital because of their ability to weaken, crack, tear down, and continuously contaminate the contents and character of the foundation we will need to effectively change our lives, to change our situations, and to become better people.

Weaknesses and cracks in our foundation will cause a collapse or major instability in whatever we are trying to build. They will keep our self-growth, our marriages, our relationships, our families, our careers, and all that we dream or desire collapsing or unstable. Again, with unresolved matters present, our lives will never be stable, secure, or strengthened enough to uphold anything that has the potential to continuously persevere, grow, and prosper over long periods of time. If we want to get to a place where we can genuinely enjoy life, matters must be resolved in ways that continue to produce and reproduce growth, courage, confidence, love, respect, honesty, and inner strength within ourselves. Maturely resolved matters will show that we have surrendered ourselves to learning from the situation while bringing some sense of peace to the situation. And as result of doing that, we are indeed journeying into becoming a better person.

Forgiveness is one way to deal with our unresolved matters. In short, forgiveness means to stop blaming and to stop feeling angered or ill-will towards someone or something for wrongs or wrongdoing in our lives. It means to stop requiring payment from or wanting to avenge a wrong. We have to forgive others if we want acts of forgiveness reciprocated to us in life. If we find it difficult for us to forgive people or to go to them and beg their pardon, we should seek counsel and the necessary tools as a means to accomplish that. Even if a lot of time has passed, if we know without a shadow of a doubt that we have wronged or caused others grief or sorrow at some point in their lives, we need to ask them for forgiveness.

In some cases, it may not be possible to ask someone for forgiveness (in the case they have died or some other dire situation that pertains to the person). It is also possible that the people whom we do ask to forgive us won't! The important thing is to do our part to resolve the matter and make things right. Make it right according to God's word, right according to love, right according to peace, and right according to life. We can't make people forgive us. We can only offer the opportunity and open the door of our hearts for forgiveness to take place.

Another important point we must consider when asking others for forgiveness is that we can't ask for forgiveness then continue to do the same things that created the hurt, sorrow, or strife in the first place! If we are sincere when we are asking God and others to forgive us, our actions and behavior should show it. If our motives behind asking for forgiveness are really honest and true, we will do whatever we can to correct actions and/or behaviors that are not supporting the words that are coming forth out of our mouths.

As we travel upon our road to becoming a better person, we must continuously make efforts to leave nothing unresolved on our part. As the bible quotes in Roman 12:18: (NIV) *If it is possible, as far as it depend on you (us), live at peace with all men.* God gives the most instrumental part to us. He wants us to do all we can to live peaceably! Our becoming better is not tied up in what others may unproductively be giving or bringing to us. But it does matter what we are productively giving of ourselves to others. I love that the scripture says "if it be possible." I love that it gives us the word "if" being that "if" is a conditional clause. I love it because it shows there is a possibility that peace will not be made in every situation. Yet, peace can definitely be made within our own selves as it pertains to the situation.

Resolving unresolved matters makes us better because we are saying to the situations, "although we have experienced what we've experienced, and we have felt whatever bad, negative, grievous, or vindictive ways we have felt, we are consciously and subconsciously acknowledging the act or matter for what it was and for what it is." We take control of the matter by consciously and subconsciously making peace with the act or matter as it is, as it was, and however it looks like it is going to be. Our acknowledgement and forgiveness does not mean we may like the situation nor like how we feel about the outcome of a situation. But, what we are gifting our hearts, our minds, and our souls with through acknowledgement and forgiveness, is a foundation where the resolving of the situations and matters can begin to trigger good a lot more than they trigger bad. They will begin to trigger joy more than they trigger pain. They will begin to trigger thankfulness, happiness, peace, and hope, more than they trigger regret, sadness, anger, and defeat. We owe it to ourselves to become all that we are destined and purposed to be. We must believe our better self is worth all the sleepless nights, all the dire and painful moments, and all the tears we may have shed in our lifetime! We must believe our better self is worth all the courage and hard work it takes to change and evolve. We must believe our better selves are worth all the challenges and perseverance it takes to live this life of becoming a better person.

Note: Like many things in life, dealing with, processing, and bringing to resolve unresolved matters takes time, patience, prayer, and a commitment to better one's self. It takes trust in God, trust in self, and trust in knowing and understanding that whatever the outcome of a particular situation might be, it is going to be okay. As long as we know we have made every effort to resolve the matter in a peaceful and productive manner, we have done the best we can do about it! We don't have to put unnecessary guilt or pressure on ourselves if the matter or situation we've tried to peacefully resolve is not at peace! We can only do what we can do and the things we cannot do, well let's just trust God with those things. We only have God's permission to be co-creators of our own lives. We should do all we can to better situations and leave the rest in the hands of the Ultimate Creator. Leave it in the hands of God.

5. Moving Through Our Experiences

There really is a place in time where we are able to step out of painful and/or unproductive situations and into enjoyable and fulfilling futures. I and many other people are living witnesses to that. It takes time and patience, but if we continue upon our journey to become a better person, and if we are putting in the efforts and good works, there will come a day when our past (and all it entailed and represented), will really be "our past!" We won't arrive at this place overnight or with one major decision. But with every new morning, and with every new decision (big or small), we can be gifted with God's goodness, with strength, with opportunities, and with the courage to take steps farther away from the things we really need to leave behind.

When we desire to experience something different in life, we must effectively move through the experiences we are already in. We must take heed to moving through our experiences in ways that does not allow the experience to keep repeating itself in negative and unproductive ways in our lives. Those are signs of being stuck in our experiences! We will stay stuck and won't move through our experiences effectively if we are refusing to grow up, refusing to take an entirely different approach, and if we are continuously trying to carry many of our old ways, our bad attitudes, our complaints, or any unnecessary baggage (burdens) along with us.

If we want to outlast our adversity and steadily move through our experiences, we must adapt to change. And all excess baggage that weighs us down mentally, emotionally, physically, or spiritually, has to be let go and left behind. If things are weighing us down financially, we may have to let certain things go in that situation also. To outlast adversity, we sometimes have to make like birds and fly high above the storms in our lives in order for us to survive them. If things are weighing us down and keeping us from taking flight off the ground, we will never be able to soar above some of our experiences in life. We won't be able to soar above them or be mobile enough to get to the other side of them.

Through a lot of my past experiences, I gave myself the best gift (through understanding myself, understanding what I could and could not do, understanding how life works, and understanding the love, patience, and mercies of God), when I gave myself permission to let go of wanting to always stand tall and control everything. I had to let go of the weight of trying to carry everything on my shoulders and the need to act as if I had to have my life all together, all the time. Letting go of those mindsets and the heavy burdens associated with them was hard and painful at first because they had become an integral part of who I was and the life I had built. They were also a part of my identity and to strip them from myself meant having to lose parts of myself. It also meant losing control of parts of my life and all I had built using those mindsets. Yes, it was hard and painful (more disappointing), but it eventually became extremely freeing and very uplifting. Though very painful and disappointing, I was no longer enslaved to self-imposed stressors and pressure. I was no longer having to be strong and no longer having to be who and what everybody else needed me to be. I was slowly learning how to just be! (I speak more about my story on letting go in topic 8, "A New Way of Life.")

Through life, many of us are taught to be strong and to keep things together no matter what is going on in our lives. When we are in our experiences, we hold on to those same mindsets of having to be strong and hold everything together. In a lot of our situations, being strong and holding everything together is not even a choice for most of us. But with growth and maturity, we learn that there are times in our experiences when we must give ourselves permission to be weak, to be hurt, to be shameful, to be wrong, and to be vulnerable in life. We must give ourselves permission to be fully exposed in the presence of our Higher Power (God). It is in these moments that God can become our covering, our protection, and our strength while hiding our weaknesses, our fragileness, and our vulnerabilities from the world. It is in these times where it is an offer to become beautifully broken and pliable in the presence of God. It is in these times that our lives can be restructured and changed forever.

While moving through our experiences, life may show us negative signs to make us think we aren't really moving forward and things are not really changing. Life may also be telling us that things aren't getting better and we aren't becoming better. But during these times we have to walk by faith (*the confidence in what we hope for and assurance about what we do not see,* [as defined in the Bible, Hebrews 11:1 NIV]), and not by sight. Hebrews 11:3 (NIV) reads: *By faith we understand that the universe was formed at God's command, so that what is seen was not made out of what was visible.*

It is God and ourselves who makes things become visible from the invisible. Things come into existence in places where they did not already exist when we keep pushing forward. Therefore, we've got to trust, believe, and know that every single day we are getting closer to the joys that lie ahead of us. Regardless of what our circumstances may look like, better days really are ahead for us. The bible confirms it in Haggai 2:9 (NIV) ... it reads: *The glory of this present house will be greater than the glory of the former house, says the Lord Almighty. And in this place I will grant peace, declared the Lord Almighty.* Things will get better! As better people, our latter days will be better than our former days. There is a rainbow after every storm and there is hope and a ray of sunshine behind every dark cloud. But we must be willing to move through our experiences to get to this place. We have to put aside our fears of doing something different and having something different in our lives. We have to put aside our fears of becoming someone different. To sum it all up, we have to step out of our comfort zones and our familiarities "our boats!"

In Matthew 14:23-31 (NIV): When Jesus bid Peter to step out of the boat and onto the water (Jesus was already walking on the water), He exemplified some great analogies for our journey of becoming a better person and moving through our experiences. The analogies are (1) in order to do what may seem seemingly impossible, we have to be connected to and trust The One who has the power to make all things possible, "God and our true selves" (2) If we continue to sit in the boat because we are afraid to confront fears and afraid to take chances, we are going to stay stuck in our experiences, "our comfort zones and our familiar places". (3) Unless we trust and step out of our comfort zones and familiar places, we will never experience the fulfillment that awaits us. And (4) if and when we began to get discouraged or distracted once we are out of our boats (and moving through our experiences), continuously trusting God, trusting our true selves, and our continuous perseverance will be able to see us through.

Don't just watch everyone else move through their experiences and become victors and overcomers. Don't just watch others accomplish great things and enjoy their lives. We are capable of doing what we need to do to live out our lives better and joyously also. When I think of stepping out of the boat, I think of stretching our limits mentally, emotionally, spiritually, and sometimes physically to become the person we desire to become. Stepping out the boat means we will have to challenge ourselves. It can be paraphrased as saying we have to take risks and may have to do things we might not want to do. We may have to make choices we don't want to make. We may even have to be displaced and uncomfortable for a while in order to get where we are trying to go. But we must keep the faith! And we must keep moving forward. We may run into a lot of stormy weather, but we must believe and know that we will eventually run into our sunshine.

The disciple Peter is a person I admire in the bible. I admire Peter's character during the time he followed and walked with Jesus because he would at least stretch his own limits. If Jesus rebuked him, he just got rebuked! For example, when Jesus told Peter that He (Jesus) was going to die, Peter told Jesus that He (Jesus) was not going to die and Peter got rebuked (reprimanded, scolded) by Jesus for saying that. And as I already briefly spoke about in "Storms help us to deal with our inner selves," when Jesus told Peter that he (Peter) would deny Him (Jesus) three times before the rooster crowed that particular day, Peter emphatically insisted to Jesus that he would never disown Him (Jesus), then turned right around that very same day and denied Jesus three times.

Through Peter's many questions and through his many trials and errors, he learned a lot about Jesus. He also ended up learning a lot about himself. After the resurrection and because of Peter's bold indiscretions and denial of Jesus, only he (Peter) was asked three times by Jesus of his love for Jesus, and asked three times to feed Jesus's sheep (his people). Only Peter got to fully experience what it felt like to be restored after blatantly denying Jesus during that time (Mark 14:26-31, John 21:15-22). Can you imagine what that must have felt like to Peter? To deny Jesus three times just as Jesus said he would! And to make the shameful and highly disappointing feeling even worse, after the third denial, Jesus turned and looked directly at Peter as to remind him and say "I told you that you would deny me three times before the rooster crowed today." I can't even imagine the depth of the piercing hurt and disappointment Peter must have felt within himself in that moment when his eyes locked in with Jesus's eyes! Just the mere guilt of it all had to be totally devastating! The bible goes on to say that Peter went out and wept bitterly (Luke 22:62 [NIV]). I would have done the same!

Some of Peter's ways reminds me of myself. I am quick to stretch my limits and step out the boat and onto the water in my life and when I do, it's either sink or swim time for me. At times I have swam, and there are times when I have sunk. But just like with Peter, God rebukes (scolds) me; and because God is merciful, He then stretches forth His hand and helps me in those sunken moments. Again, if we want to experience something different in life, we have to be courageous enough to step out of our boats. I would rather have God have to help me and say "Chavelle you wasn't supposed to do that or go that particular way," rather than hear Him say, "Chavelle, you did absolutely nothing to help yourself!" For all that awaits us on the other side of storms, struggles, and our experiences, we have to be willing to stretch our limits in life. And we first help ourselves by being courageous enough to step out of our boats.

Effectively moving through our experiences will usher us into a more productive life. When faced with future experiences, a productive life will allow us to have the experience, the acceptance of the experience, and the satisfaction or dissatisfaction of it in a way that will continue to propel us forward. A productive life does not allow us to stay stuck in the experience or in the shock of the experience. Certain situations may still be able to take us by surprise, but a productive life will give us quality and tranquil time to gather ourselves. Once we gather ourselves, a productive life will then gracefully help us to move along at a pace that is good and healthy for us.

While moving through our experiences, it is also important not to keep walls built up in our lives. These are the walls that may have been built because we were wronged, hurt, or mistreated by others. We can't keep those type walls up because in our determination to shut people out and not ever go through that experience ever again, we also succeed at shutting ourselves in with the feelings and emotions relating to the experience. And when we shut ourselves in with the feeling and emotions of our situations and our experiences, we also shut ourselves in with all the hurt, pain, disappointments, and terrible memories of the experience.

Be mindful not to build walls with "self" standing behind them! Continuous and lengthy isolation is not good for the mind, body, or the soul. Besides, no one has to hurt us if we are boarded behind our walls hurting ourselves! We continue to hurt ourselves by holding on to false senses of safety and security. We also self-medicate ourselves when we are behind the walls we've built. That's all dangerous because when our false senses of being safe and secure diminishes (and one day they will), the hurt and pain we self-medicated will also return. And if we aren't careful, the hurt, pain, and disappointments could possibly leave us more devastated than we were when they first occurred. Here are a few examples of self-medicating ourselves:

- Turning to alcoholic beverages, food, or un-prescribed drugs for comfort
- Abusing the use of pills (anti-depressants)
- Running into the arms (or bed) of another person mainly for self-esteem purposes
- Living financially above our means
- Showing no emotions or feelings: passiveness
- Being overly emotional or aggressive
- Being too busy ... all the time

- Isolating ourselves from others and outside activities
- Being negative/cynical
- Blaming others and not accepting full responsibility for our lives
- Constantly blaming and not forgiving ourselves for the things we have control over, and things we do not have control over
- Constantly focusing on poor choices we have made in life

To deal with our agonies in any of the ways given in the examples above will only have negative effects on ourselves and the ones around us. They may seemingly help get us through our experiences, but we will soon find out that the fix was only temporary. And because the fix is temporary, we may soon find ourselves back into the exact same or similar experiences. We can't heal ourselves or put ourselves in a position to be healed if we are self-medicating ourselves and are barricaded behind our built-up walls. Life and light of the world has to be able to shine through our experiences in order for us to receive healing that will move us through our experiences in healthy ways.

There is something else of extreme importance we should grasp when it comes to moving through our experiences. We don't want to move through our experiences too quickly and not receive the blessings in them. Many of our experiences won't feel good, but that's exactly why we should not want to leave that place empty handed. Sometimes we have to marinate long enough in the experience to be sure we will come out on the other side of it with undeniably life changing results. In Genesis 32:22-29, when Jacob was having his experience and wrestled with the Angel of the Lord, the Angel of the Lord touched Jacob's hip to push it out of place. At that particular point in the wrestling match, Jacob KNEW he was at a permanent disadvantage for life. He also knew he was about to face some of his biggest fears and challenges. And now with an disjointed hip, Jacob knew he NEEDED God! He knew he could not go on with the rest of his life without the help, comfort, and strength of his higher power. So what did Jacob do in that tragic, humbling, defeated, broken, and helpless moment? Jacob holds on to God and tells Him, *I'm not letting you go until you bless me.* Let me repeat that. Jacob says to the Angel of the Lord (God), *"I'M NOT LETTING YOU GO UNTIL YOU BLESS ME!"*

Jacob had already experienced a lot of agony in his life. But now He was about to face anguish on a whole different level. This one was heartfelt and beloved. This one would make him face himself and the root of all his dirty deeds. Jacob was returning to his homeland and was about to face his twin brother Esau whom he had cheated out of both his birthright and his inheritance. Because of that, Esau hated Jacob and vowed to kill him as soon as their sick father "Isaac" had died. As a result, Jacob fled his homeland and was separated from his family for more than 20 years. He was now returning home and knew he would have to face his long-time enemy, the man he significantly cheated twice! And although Jacob was a changed man, he greatly feared his brother Esau and was severely distressed about having to face him. Jacob was praying and hoping for a change within the situation pertaining to him and his brother, but, IF HE HAD TO FIGHT - he had previously prepared himself to do so.

Fast forward ... after wrestling with the Angel of the Lord, and now that Jacob's hip was somewhat broken, his previous preparation to fight on his own, and for his life, and for the life of his family, had also been broken. He was now disabled in his own strength! He now knew, without any doubt, that the rest of his life, the life of his family, and the generations to come under him, gravely DEPENDED on the mercy and blessing of the Lord. His brother Esau, and the rest of his future, was nothing he wanted to face or could face without help from God, so he desperately held on to God pleading for God to bless him. And what did God do? Genesis 32:26-29 reads (NIV) *Then the man said, "Let me go, for it is daybreak." But Jacob replied, "I will not let you go unless you bless me." The man asked him, "What is your name?" "Jacob'" he answered. Then the man said, "Your name will no longer be Jacob, but Israel, because you have struggled with God and with humans and have overcome." Jacob said, "Please tell me your name." but He replied, "Why do you ask my name?" THEN HE BLESSED HIM (JACOB) THERE.* God saw Jacob's brokenness, his persistence, his desperation, and his NEED for a life changing existence and God blessed Jacob right then and there!

Note: I mentioned in the earlier part of "moving through our experiences" how we must get to a place where we are beautifully broken and pliable before the Lord. I mentioned how the Lord then becomes our strength and changes and restructures our lives. Like with Jacob, sometimes God has to disable us from our own strength in order to help us! Sometimes He has to break us from whatever "little" strength we have left in order to change us. And once we are put in a helpless and desperate position like Jacob, and once we realize there is absolutely nothing we can do about anything in our own strength, we too should desperately hold on to the Lord until He blesses us. Do not leave your situations (experiences) without the blessing! I repeat, DO NOT leave your situations (experiences) without the blessing! After wrestling and struggling with God, other people, and life itself, a blessing is humbly warranted and deserved in the end! Grab God and don't let HIM go until He blesses you!

6. Self

Acknowledging "self" on our journey to becoming a better person is of significance. Self is important and it is time to discover who self truly is as well as begin to invest in self! Self obviously has his/her own needs and wants. Self's needs and wants must be identified, nurtured, and preferably by "self" first. When we know what we want and need, we can communicate that to others. But in order to know those things, we must become aware of every little detail about ourselves. We have to know our selves inside and out. We need to know everything about who we are, who we aren't, and if we are open to being adjustable. We need to know what we need in our lives, what we don't need in our lives, and what we can accept, can't accept or can and can't tolerate. We must know what makes us happy, what makes us sad, what makes us thrive, and what brings us down. Know what makes us comfortable, what makes us uncomfortable and what it is that we need and want to offer to ourselves, to others, and possibly to the world.

Throughout life, we are often making deposits into the lives of others, but we usually don't take the time to make deposits into our own lives. It is not uncommon for us to live out our lives being sick, damaged, wounded, broke, broken, and unhappy people while attempting to deposit healing, wholeness, happiness and wealth into the lives of others. In always taking care of and supporting others, we ignore, are unaware of, or we are too busy and too tired to attend to the many cracks, bruises, and unmet needs we harbor in our own lives. Sometimes, even if a void or unmet need of our own is brought to our attention, we continue to ignore it, or put a temporary fix on it and tell ourselves "as long as everybody else is happy and taken care of, then we ourselves will be alright." We bleed (and sometimes heavily bleed), yet attend to the cuts and wounds of others first. We suffer and allow ourselves to slowly die while making sure others have everything they need to live.

When we don't take the time to properly take care of self, we won't be able to continuously and properly take care of others no matter how hard we try. Life will eventually catch up with us and we will begin to see and feel how ignoring our own needs and how ignoring our own life, have begun to negatively affect us. It is mandatory that we take the time to regularly take inventory of self and allow self to be discovered, expressed, nurtured, healed, and fulfilled. Once we come into this knowledge, there should be no more living out our lives as damaged, wounded, broke, broken, and unhappy people. We can never give our best, if we are not at our best. And who will ever know what our best really is if we don't know! It's time for self to be placed into his or her rightful position, and that's in response to our spouses, parents, children, friends, businesses, and all that pulls on us and continuously need a part of who we are.

Self in his or her rightful position will help bring balance to our lives. We need balance to keep us centered in life. Also, being in our rightful position (as better people), gives us a magnetic power that's capable of attracting and pulling good things toward ourselves. It does not matter if the rightful position represents us being the best parent we can be, being the best friend we can be, being the best spouse, the best worker, child, designer, stylist, cook, baker, doctor, lawyer, speaker, teacher, housewife etc. Whatever our rightful positions are in life, if we are positioned there as better people, the position is going to reap some personal benefits and some good in our lives.

Look in the mirror and ask yourself, do I like and love the person I see staring back at me? And is the person who is staring back at me getting what he or she truly deserves out of life? Am I giving the best I have to offer to myself? Am I giving myself the love and respect I need? Am I choosing to be happy? In order for our lives to express love, growth, change, beauty, character, and all that adds to our true being, self has to play an important role in it. And self at his or her best will have to come to the forefront of our lives. People will never give us or continue to give to us, what we aren't willing to give to and demand from ourselves. When we are aware of all that self needs to thrive, we then have the information and the power to make the necessary changes to better self. When we can consistently make changes to better self, we are then on the path to becoming better people. Self has to matter! Self "absolutely" has to matter!

Note: Because I am championing taking interest in self and making self a priority, allow me to clarify that there is a difference between making self a priority, and being selfish! I am NOT referring to putting "self" first in a selfish manner. Selfish is defined as a person, action, or motive lacking consideration for others. Selfish people are filled with discussions about themselves (me, I, and always me and I). They never take the time to truly listen to what someone else might be going through or what others may be thinking, feeling, or have to say. When in the presence of and dealing with selfish people, a person never really feels heard or feel like their voice or issues are of importance to the selfish person. So in these type situations, these people "selfish ones" must learn how to STOP only thinking of self and learn how to think about the needs, wants, and feelings of others.

Sometimes life has to teach selfish people how to take the focus off of them and pay attention to someone else. If a selfish person desires change, they must want to be enlightened as to how their selfishness and their small worlds of me, me, I, and me, negatively (and painfully) affects the lives of others. Again, I am not referring to putting "self" first in a manner that makes a person arrogant, entitled, and ONLY thinking about themselves.

Instead, I am referring to putting "self" first in a way that makes a person humble, appreciative, thankful, and able to love themselves and life in ways that will equip them to hopefully want to help and share with others out of the wonderful overflow of who they truly are!

7. Relationships

We need relationships in our lives. We can't become better people without them. We won't be healed, whole, and happy people without having others to interact and share our lives with. What we must take into account is the type of relationships we need around us in order for our lives to be healthy, functional, and able to grow. It is important to know what role each person plays and what role we are playing also. Is the relationship helping us, hindering us, or hurting us? Is it stagnant; or does it inspire love, change, and growth?

In an online article entitled "Why Personal Relationships Are Important" (written by expert contributor Mary Jo Kreitzer, a PhD, RN) and presented online through "Taking Charge of your Health and Wellbeing (a website created by the University of Minnesota)," it reads "Healthy relationships are a vital component of health and wellbeing. There is compelling evidence that strong relationships contribute to a long, healthy, and happy life. Conversely, the health risks from being alone or isolated in one's life are comparable to the risks associated with cigarette smoking, blood pressure, and obesity." The article goes on to say that "healthy relationships can help you live longer, deal with stress, be healthier, and feel richer." This is just a summary of what the article says. If you would like to read more on the article you can find the reference in the back of this book.

Before we can establish good, productive, healthy, and valuable relationships with other people, we must establish that type of relationship with "self" first. Remember, we can't give others what we do not have access to in our own lives! To become better people, we must educate ourselves on the necessary tools needed to become a better person and to have a better life. Once we have the necessary tools, we must do the work to implement those tools by making the necessary changes and sacrifices it takes to bring what we desire into our lives. And hopefully, healthy and growing relationships are one of those desires.

Good and healthy relationships do not feel pressured. They are not envious and jealous of each other. They do not try to control, disrespect, or manipulate the other person's life or his or her boundaries. Good and healthy relationships don't always take and never give anything back. These relationships are patient, kind, and understanding. They support and will encourage our walk forward in life. They inspire us and give us a sense of trust and comfort. They are flourishing and prosperous. Good and healthy relationships create order, harmony, and balance. They exemplify a willingness to help one another, to protect one another, to hold the other up, and to even help carry the other if needed. Good and healthy relationships communicate with one another, listen to one another, and resolve issues in love.

It is very important for me to know that the people who are closest to me want me to win in life! I need to know without any doubt that they want me living life to my fullest potential and being the best me I can possibly be. In any good and healthy relationship, a person should feel free enough in the relationship to be who they truly are as long as who they truly are is not hurting, disrespecting, or bringing harm to themselves or others. A person should be able to make the decision to become a better self if they choose to. They should not have to feel as if their growth will possibly threaten and isolate the ones closest to them in a negative way. We want our change for the better to be celebrated and embraced, not put down and ridiculed. If a relationship is not supportive of any of these good things, then we should really reevaluate the relationship and possibly make some hard and painful decisions about it.

Family

What do families bring to our sense of well-being? They actually bring a lot to it. I love my family and I love relationships when it comes to family. Family gives us a sense of who we are, where we belong, and why we look the way we do. Understanding our family dynamics can help us get to the root of some of our struggles in life. Understanding family dynamics helps us to identify some of our mindsets, behaviors, and the reasons why we believe certain things and do certain things. Family plays an important role in setting the foundation for who we are and who we are to become. Family can set the foundation for what is to become of the generations that follow us. Good or bad, our families represent a part of us. They represent where we have been and help set the tone for where we want to go in life.

In an online web article written by the American Psychological Association discussing Family and Relationships, it reads "At every stage of life, our relationships and families presents us with both joys and challenges. Learning to manage stress, to understand our own emotions and behaviors, and to communicate effectively can help strengthen our own emotional health, as well as our connections to the important people in our lives."

Our connections to our families are essential. If we aren't able to connect with them and others, how will we be able to connect with God, with healing, with love, with wholeness, or with happiness? How will we be able to connect to a better version of ourselves? Life, God, healing, wholeness, happiness, and relationships all relate to and connect with one another. When there is a disconnection with the people who are supposed to be near and dear to us like our mothers, fathers, sisters, brothers, children, aunts, uncles etc., we are disconnected with the totality, the fullness, and the order of life. That's not good because if it is one thing we will learn during our lifetime, it is the fact that we need our families. We especially need each other in the appointed roles God positioned us to fulfill.

Because of life's struggles and the fact that some people are not able to fulfill their appointed roles in life, others sometimes have to take on the responsibility of being more than their appointed role in the lives of others and the ones they love. For example, some Moms have to play the roles of both Mom and Dad. Some Dads have to play the roles of Dad and Mom. Grandparents have to play the roles of being Grandparent, Mom, and Dad. Step-parents are playing the roles of Mom or Dad. There are aunts and uncles who raise their nieces and nephews like their own children. There are cousins raising other cousins, etc. The point I'm trying to make clear here is "we need our families!" We need that bond and the love and support that should be readily available from them.

Now in some cases, we may have to sometimes separate ourselves from family if their actions or behaviors are inappropriate, or are bringing unnecessary stress, drama, disrespect, and pain into our lives. If separating ourselves from them has to happen, hopefully that separation won't carry us to a place where we will have to totally shut them out of our lives. If it does, hopefully they will be able to get the help and understanding they need in order to see and comprehend what is causing the unwanted issue. And prayerfully, if (and after), change, respect, understanding, and communication are accomplished, the family connection can be restored.

At the end of the day, family will be one of the most valuable and important relationships in our lives. Bloodlines can't be changed and it is actually nice knowing we aren't alone in this big world. Family relationships require us to have a little more patience and understanding because of it being family. But like all relationships, they sometimes require boundaries and a level of respect in hopes that individuals will grow and mature to a place where we can eventually communicate and be at peace.

Note: As we become better people, we inherit the power to change things in our lives that our families may represent, but may not be good for us or the family we want to raise and nurture. If that's our situation, know that it's ok to change things because none of us are perfect. As we journey through life, we will see that some family characteristics and traits aren't good for us to carry into our futures. Some things will need to be changed and some things will be best left behind. Through all we go through in life, friends don't always have to be friends, but family will always be family!

Relating to Our Children

As I write on this topic, please know I am aware that all childhoods consist of many different dynamics and we all do the best we can as parents and children. We all navigate through parenthood and childhood according to the tools and circumstances we are given to work with. My reason for writing on this topic is mainly to relate it to our journey of "becoming" a better person for ourselves. My opinions are not written to judge anyone's parenting skills or any childhoods. Taking all the different dynamics of parenting and childhoods in consideration, I'm mainly sharing my practical and overall opinion from lessons learned and experience as a parent. I'm not writing on this topic to be right or matter of fact. With that being said, I will now continue with this topic.

Parenting does not come with a manual so as parents, we truly do the best we can with what we have to offer our children. Sometimes what we have to offer our children is good enough, and honestly, sometimes it's not good enough! But, as parents, it is our job to raise our children, protect our children, provide for our children, and prepare our children for life in the best ways we possibly can. That is our responsibility! It is also our responsibility to make our children feel loved, safe, secure, confident, important, and respected. If we refuse our children any of these needs, they will either get the needs fulfilled in other ways, or just continue to lack the needs as they grow into adulthood.

Because I want to keep this topic light and not get into any dynamics (simply because that can require counsel), I will just say that as parents, we won't always get it exactly right and parenting can be a learning experience for us parents, as well as for the children we are parenting. I believe every parent needs help and guidance from God when it comes to parenting and relating to our children. We aren't all-knowing like He is. And because every child is different, God's grace, wisdom, love, and guidance will always be "the better way" when it comes to parenting.

It is important that we are able to relate to our children to some extent. All children need parents whom they feel they can talk to, who will listen to them, try to understand them, and who will give them the tools, time, and space they need to grow and develop into their own persons. When we are not relatable parents, we sometimes ignore our children's own individuality and their own natural gifts and talents. Instead, we become the parents who pressure them into what we want them to become. We pressure them because we want them to succeed. We might pressure them because we don't want them to make the same mistakes we did in life. We pressure them because we are trying to live out our own unfulfilled dreams through our children. And sometimes we pressure them because we have a "look" (an image), we don't want tarnished by something we feel they may be doing or representing.

There is absolutely nothing wrong with us parents wanting our children to succeed in life. But pressuring them to fulfill an unfulfilled dream of ours, or pressuring them because of a fairytale "look" or an image we are presenting to the public, well, that can be very frustrating, depressing, and devastating to our children. In this day and time, children are overwhelmed with everyday issues themselves like school, grades, friends, no friends, sports, clubs, peer pressure, college, and just being a child/teenager. Some children truly have their own fair share of very real drama, real struggles and real obstacles "family dynamics" to overcome and deal with in life. With all the issues some are faced with today, we should not underestimate or disrespect their need for time, patience, understanding, and space to process and work through all that goes on in their day to day living. They are our children but they are people too.

It is also important for our children to find their own voices and utilize their own minds during the time they are under our care. They need to be able to get in touch with their own thoughts, their own feelings, their own expressions, and their own dreams for their lives. They need to be able to recognize an issue, be able to process that issue, and experience the results and consequences of what having a voice in situations of life can do while they are under our care. Of course, as parents, our job would definitely be to set boundaries on the extent of them having that voice, making decisions, and the amount of time and space they are given. But with a little trust, and with moderate and realistic responsibilities (along with our rules and regulations), we should be open to giving our children a little freedom to properly learn from life, mature, and become their own person.

While they're learning how to recognize, process situations, and make decisions, we should definitely be there to help steer them in a better direction if need be. Not better direction because their decisions need to absolutely please and satisfy us, but a better direction because we are the adults and possibly have the experience and wisdom to know what problems and consequences some decisions can bring into their lives.

Also, I have heard many parents say things like, "I'm not going to be my child's friend; and what I say they are going to do!" Or "that is what's wrong with the world today; parents want to be their children's friends instead of being parents!" I do understand why some parents feel this way. When parenting, if certain disciplines are not taken heed to and respected, the parent/child dynamic can get out of control. But, if authority, voices, and disciplinary actions are heeded to and respected, and if positions in the household are respected, a parent will be able to feel and know that there will be times in our children's lives where we can't always be forceful, all-knowing, and dominant parents. There will be times when our children will just need a friend or a soft place inside of the parent.

I agree there should never be a question of who is the parent and who is the child floating around in the atmosphere of the home. But I also believe as parents to today's children, we have to learn how to keep our authoritative parental roles while still being able to become friends, confidants, mentors, and role models for our children. We won't have to worry about them crossing the line of being a child to thinking they are the parent(s) or an adult if healthy boundaries are set, respect is upheld on both ends, and just consequences are applied to out of control and disrespectful actions and behaviors.

Again, keep in mind that I am only a parent. I am not a psychologist, psychiatrist, nor am I any type of counselor. These are merely my opinions and insights from my own experiences that I am presenting to you. Our children need our love, our patience, and our willingness to allow them to grow and mature into themselves. And because we were children once, they need us to be somewhat relatable. By all means and in any case, LOVE YOUR CHILDREN! Show and tell them you love them!

Note: Whether our children feel they can come to us for conversations or certain resources will be based entirely upon the kind of relationships we have built with them and the person we/they are. If they don't feel they can trust us, depend on us, or is being heard by us, they won't be eager for discussions, advice, or any type of comfort. Nevertheless, as I said earlier, parenting does not come with a manual. And just like other responsibilities in life, it sometimes has to be figured out.

Bad/Unhealthy Relationships

Bad and unhealthy relationships will drain the life out of us. When a relationship is FILLED with toxic behaviors, drop it and run in the opposite direction of it! Relationships should represent love, help, support, and compassion. Not suffering, cruelty, and a whole lot of disrespect, drama, and indifferences. Suffer for the sake of lessons learned in a situation and becoming wiser and better; not for the sake of being totally denied and disrespected over and over and over again. Don't set yourself up to play the martyr for anybody! Please know that unless major changes are willing to be made in bad and unhealthy relationships, the relationship remains the same or gets worse!

Life has much more to offer us than being in bad and unhealthy relationships ... so much more! I know God can change people who may be considered bad, toxic, or difficult people in bad or unhealthy relationships. But no one should have to feel scared, stuck, constantly miserable, or feel they have to make excuses and uphold the relationship by lying about what they are really dealing with behind closed doors. Please get help, knowledge, and understanding on how to deal with a situation like that. I'm not speaking about relationships that are going through growing pains and normal life challenges. Nor am I speaking about relationships that have disagreements and experience some bumps in the road. I'm speaking on relationships that are downright degrading. Don't stay in a relationship that can be dangerous to you and/or dangerous to your children mentally, emotionally, spiritually, or physically.

I may sound a bit aggressive on this topic, but know in the deepest of my heart, I am not against anything! If a person loves where there are in life - good, bad, or indifferent, there's nothing I, or anyone else, can do about that. What I'm standing up for is our rights! We must honor, exercise, and uphold our rights to choose, our rights to be heard, and our rights to live a life that is authentic, peaceful, pleasing, and fulfilling with love, dignity, happiness, and respect. No one and no relationship should be able to take those precious things away from us. Rather than give up our rights to happiness, love, security, freedom, and what we want to experience in life, it would be far better to give up the bad/unhealthy relationship.

With that being said, never allow people who don't really know anything about you or your relationships to make final decisions for you. No one walks in your particular shoes but you, and no one knows exactly all that goes on in anyone's life except the ones whose life it is. Other people ways of dealing with issues (even the same issues) are not always "the way" we should deal with our own. So make decisions based on what you feel and think is right and safe for you and your family. Don't make final decisions based on what others may have to say, think, or feel about "your" situation. Definitely make safety a priority in all bad and unhealthy relationships.

Note: Relationships are essential but require work and effort. Unfortunately, some people don't fully understand the responsibilities and accountability it takes to maintain committed, loving, respectful and healthy relationships. Those are things that might not had been taught or displayed in some homes so it's something that some people never had the privilege of witnessing or being aware of. Some of us have no idea what sacrificing and compromising for the betterment in a relationship really entails. Then sometimes we don't know how or when we should bring balance to a relationship or when our acts of sacrificing and compromising becomes too much or is too little. Most of us have to figure out through life and maturity how to truly love, support, protect, and strengthen one another.

As we become better people, key elements can be learned and relationships can grow, thrive, and be restored. Not all relationships may be restorable, but in situations where hearts are softened and there isn't any ongoing disrespect or abuse of any kind, relationships have a chance of becoming something new and something different. Please do not live life alone, hollow, and saddened. Take the time to build good, loving, supportive, respectful, and healthy relationships with others.

The
Buildup

8. A New Way of Life

Do you really believe you could be a better person? Do you believe life could be stable, peaceful, fun, joyous, and prosperous after months, or even years, of terrible mishaps, misery, grief, anger, sorrow, debts and defeats? I hope you believe it! When we are in our experiences, it's often hard to see anything but our misery, our frustrations, and our lack or despair. We hope and pray we will find reasons to smile, to laugh, and to be happy again. We hope and pray that through somebody, or through something - a great change, a great blessing, or a great miracle is soon to come. We long for something different and desire to be in a place where we can really enjoy life. We desire a place where some of our wants, but especially our needs are consistently met. We desire a place where our hearts, our minds, and our souls can be free, happy, satisfied, and at peace.

Something I am personally familiar with is the fact that sometimes a person can struggle so much and for so long in life until all he or she knows is how to struggle (mentally, emotionally, financially, or spiritually). When a person struggles in life, it gives them a sense of always having just enough or barely enough to do the things in life they need or want to do. Financially, I lived that life for years! I wasn't destitute or anything and I afforded myself a pretty decent lifestyle, but putting both my sons through high school, then college, and making all those sacrifices as a single woman was definitely a struggle for me. I worked hard and hustled to a fault as I tried to fulfill their financial needs and obligations as well as my own financial needs and obligations. I made it work, but it always kept me in a place of having just enough to make it work. My sons are two years apart and they both were in college at the same time. If you know what it's like to have one child in college, then you can totally understand where I'm coming from having had two in college simultaneously.

For approximately 13 years, I worked extra hard with no real rest or vacation time. In those years, I maneuvered with just enough to comfortably stay on top of everything. Those were some financially tight years and after my last son graduated from college, I was happily and thankfully looking for change and a new beginning in so many ways and in so many areas in my life. I was looking for change but the change and a new beginning was not manifesting. For some reason, I was still maneuvering with just enough; still working hard, still tired, and still very much in need of rest and a good vacation!

One day, as I was complaining about being extra tired and always "doing" something, it took a very good and honest friend telling me I had gotten used to struggling and making things hard for myself to make an "aha" (lightbulb, epiphany) moment appear in my head. Her saying that struck me deeply the moment it came out of her mouth! I immediately knew in my heart she was telling me the absolute truth. I was enlightened and over the next few days of self-evaluation, I understood my situation and realized I had a struggling mindset and struggling aspects about myself. After 13 years of having just enough financial means and doing what I could to make life happen, struggling was definitely what I had become familiar with. And because I was familiar with it, I subconsciously kept myself financially strapped. I kept putting myself in situations that made me struggle because it felt right and comfortable to me.

Wow, isn't that something! To actually have to admit that "struggling" felt right and comfortable to me! Yet, that was my truth. I look back on that time now and I'm absolutely amazed at how powerful our mindsets are. I'm amazed at how our mindsets will definitely create and control our reality. We will have whatever our mindsets negatively encompass as long as the mindsets are familiar to us and goes unnoticed! Through examining my decisions in life, my mindsets, and my reality, I realized I honestly had no idea how to live life freely or how to just simply be. And because I didn't know how to live life freely or just be, I knew I needed a new mindset, new thoughts, new actions, and new behaviors to go along with the new beginning and new way of life I desired. I needed to re-co-create my reality! A struggler doesn't always have to be a struggler and I was determined to free myself from that captivity. I was determined to get cleansed from those defeating mindsets, decisions and behaviors. I became destined and determined to transition to the other side of struggle and living life less than I was created to live life. I became destined and determined to live my best life!

Becoming a better self is about discovery and self-discovery. It is about change and going through the motions of embracing, discarding, accepting truth, forgiving self, asking for forgiveness, healing, hope, and having faith (not necessarily in that order). It is about creatively and selflessly becoming the center and foundation of all we want to receive and offer to ourselves, to our loved ones, and eventually offer to the world.

When becoming a better person, change and new beginnings can feel so scary. They feel both wonderful and scary at the same time. When we begin to change, the nature and complacency of situations and relationships in our lives begins to change also. Some people will support our new journey and some will resist and resent our wanting to "change" and become better and somewhat different people. But we can't let how others feel stop us from growing, maturing, and discovering our true self. We should never be made to feel guilty or less than about wanting to become a better and different version of ourselves. We should feel good about implementing good and positive changes into our lives.

Our new way of life is about God and us working together to create an atmosphere and a life that gives us more than enough to satisfy and meet our needs, our wants, and our desires. Not only are we creating an atmosphere and a life that will fully meet our needs, wants and desires; we are also creating a life that will give us an overflow of all the good and positive things we desire. As better people, we are to give others out of the abundance of our cup that runneths over. We can't give out of a cup that is always empty; nor can we give much out of a cup that is less than half full. As I mentioned earlier, we also can't give others what we do not possess. We can't give what we don't have access to for our own selves. And we definitely can't give to others if we are living a life that is always struggling or highly lacking in some form be it financially, mentally, spiritually or emotionally.

When I think of a better life, I think of abundant living. When I think of abundant living, I think about having the resources to get our needs met and having the heart, resources, and desire to help other people get their needs met as well. Abundant living puts us in a position to live in abundant hope and in service to our selves and to others. I have hope and I pray that the way I live my life will eventually add to the lives of those around me. I desire to have characteristics that are to be trusted, admired, and looked up to by whoever crosses my path. God created all things to LIVE and if "self" is always in a state of unhappiness, struggle, or survival, I feel it is safe to say that self is indeed living far below its intended purpose and potential. Jesus came so that we may have LIFE and have it MORE ABUNDANTLY (John 10:10)! Therefore, life is to be lived not loathed! Are you living, surviving, or loathing?

Deuteronomy Chapter 28, verses 3-8 (NIV) sums up abundant living the best. It reads: *Blessed shalt thou be in the city, and blessed shalt thou be in the field. Blessed shall be the fruit (children and spiritual children) of thy body, and the fruit of thy ground (all that we plant in the world), and the fruit of thy cattle (whatever we own will produce more of its kind), the increase of the kine and the flocks of thy sheep. Blessed shall thou be when thou comest in, and blessed shall thou be when thou goest out. The Lord shall cause thine enemies that rise up against thee to be smitten (defeated) before thy face: they shall come out against thee one way, and flee before thee seven ways. The Lord shall command the blessing upon thee in thy storehouses, and in all that thou setteth thine hand unto; and He shall bless thee in the land which the Lord thy God giveth thee.*

If those scriptures don't say it all, I don't know any other way to convince you that a better you, a better life, a new beginning, a new way of life, and abundant living is possible in our lives! God wants to bless His people and nothing can determine or measure the extent of our abundance or destiny in life but our selves. God is clearly telling us that we can be blessed in the cities and blessed in the fields. We can be blessed coming in and blessed going out. He says everything we put our hands to shall be blessed. That our children and our children's children (this includes any spiritual children we may have) shall be blessed. God says the fruit of the ground, meaning all the good and productive things we sow/plant in life, shall be blessed. There are so many blessings tied up in those scriptures! Lastly, the scriptures say, we shall be blessed in the land which the Lord our God gives to us and if you are like me, you want to know where that land of blessings is! Because like me, you want to experience ALL God has for us. You want the new beginning, the better place, the new way of life, the better life, and ALL the Blessings of God!

Note: I hope and pray you trust and believe that a new way of life and new beginnings exist and can be birthed and manifested through your own life. I hope and pray you are convinced and confident in knowing that through God, we have the power, the courage, and the strength inside of us to change our reality and our destiny! Information and opportunities are readily available for those who desire something good and different in their lives. I pray you will never give up along your journey of becoming a better you!

9. Life's Treasures

Two associates of mine often revealed to me how they just wanted to be happy. They always complained about NOT being happy. I specifically asked both of them what was happiness to them and their response was, "I don't know!" Of course the next questions I asked them were, "If you don't know what happiness is, how will you know it if you find it? How will you know what it looks like if it presented itself to you? And how do you know if happiness even exists?" If we can't define what happiness is for our own lives, we will probably never be happy. And not only do we need to know what we consider happiness to be, we have to open ourselves up to receive happiness when the opportunities present themselves to us.

We all have dreams and purpose within ourselves that can lead to us experiencing and having a different kind of life. Let's call these dreams and purpose our imaginary doors within. All doors on our paths to becoming a better person must be unlocked and opened from the inside of our selves. No one can get inside of our bodies and unlock and open these special doors for us. Therefore, becoming a better person really will take a conscious effort from self! Once the doors are opened to change, to life, to a guiding light and to love, there are treasures along the way that can be picked up and stored in our hearts and minds.

These treasures will help us along our journey. Once we recognize the importance of having these treasures and begin to implement them into our daily living, we are on our way to becoming the better people we desire to be. Below are six treasures I have personally implemented into my own life and would like to share with you.

Treasure (1)

Positive Thinking

We've all heard, "if we change our thinking, we can change our lives." I totally agree with that statement. Our thoughts and beliefs create our reality! Even the bible says, "For as he thinks in his heart, so is he" (Proverbs 23:7). Thinking positively has the power to take us into places we have dared to dream about. What I love about a person who thinks positively is the fact that they don't need others to think positive for them in order to achieve their goals or live their dreams. It is always great to have other people to believe in and encourage us. But even if a positive person does not have other people to believe in and encourage them, they are still able to encourage themselves and accomplish great things. Because of their persistence, dedication, and commitment to the work and to what they believe about themselves, positive people will always rise to the occasion. Even when faced with setbacks and difficulties, a positive person will not easily be stopped.

Being able to live our dreams and reach our goals will only become our reality when we are willing to think positive and self-motivate ourselves to continuously work towards achieving those things. It may seemingly take a while but plank by plank we can build a ladder to our success. We can build a ladder to a better us. And we can build a ladder to our new way of life. This is what positive thinking does for us. It gives us the strength and the will power to keep persevering, to keep moving forward, and to keep becoming a better person.

I will never forget the year my youngest son tried out for his middle school basketball team (for a second time). He did not make the team the year before and was very emotionally upset about it. Up until that first year when he tried out for the team, he had never showed an interest in sports. So now knowing he was interested, he and I decided we would sign him up to play for a recreational team where everyone on the team would get a chance to participate. By participating on a recreational team, he would learn some basketball skills and get an idea of what playing basketball was really like. I figured it would help prepare him to possibly try out again the following year. Well, a year had passed and there he was again trying out for the middle school basketball team. In all honesty, I still felt he had no chance of making the middle school team and could use one more year playing at the recreational center.

I remember how I had already started giving him pep talks about how "not" making the team was going to be okay. I remember telling him how playing another year on the recreational team would help him learn more skills and get more experience. I also remember he would ALWAYS say to me, "Mom, I am going to make that team!" He truly believed that with his whole heart! Because he truly believed he was going to make the team and was so determined and adamant about it, I remember thinking how his thinking and beliefs was only making the situation harder for me! I figured since I was going to have to be the one to comfort and console him when his little heart was broken (again), that I should do everything I could to prepare him for the heartbreak. So I thought!

Well guess what, my son made that middle school basketball team! That was a huge eye opener for me. My son making the team that year taught me so much about faith, hard work, and the power of positive thinking! No matter what I said, he did not allow it to deter or distract him from his work ethics and positive thoughts. And because of that, he was able to change his situation and accomplish his goal. He did all that without the encouragement of his mother! I must admit I felt really bad afterwards for not believing in him and his ability to follow up on what he thought and believed in his heart. But he taught me what the power of determination and positive thinking could do; especially in the face of nay-sayers and unbelievers.

Remember I spoke of having our needs met in abundance so we may give out of our cup that runneths over to others? Well, by my son having an overflow of positivity in his life, his positivity was able to flow out of his cup and into mine. To this day, his positive thinking still exist and inspires me as I watch him navigate through life and excel in the things he is determined to do. I truly love that about him and am grateful for the lesson learned.

Positive thinking will help us soar into greater heights. It can also help us create a way out of negative things like depression, grief, disappointments, despair, and lack. Positive thinking releases positive energy into the universe and keeps the world breathing and full of life (hope and happiness). If we are willing to put faith, works, and perseverance behind our positive thinking, there is no limit to what we can achieve; especially if what we are trying to achieve is in the will of God for our lives. If it's in the will of God for us and we can believe it, then we can certainly achieve it! We can exercise and build our power of positive thinking by making an effort to always think positive.

Note: Not only did my son make the middle school basketball team that year, he went on to play basketball all through his high school years. His high school team even won a District Championship his junior year! By the end of my son's high school basketball era, his high school coach was quoted saying "**No better defender,**

competitor, and leader have I ever coached" about my son. That made me very proud. And to think, his basketball journey all started with "his" positive thinking!

Treasure (2)

Acknowledge True Beauty

Our true beauty is the essence of who we are spiritually, emotionally, and mentally. True beauty has nothing to do with race, the color of our skin, or the physique of our bodies. It has nothing to do with our financial status, our titles, our cultures, or our accomplishments in life. True beauty represents something entirely different. It represents the nature of who we are. It is defined by our attitudes, our intentions, our motives, our thoughts, our character, our actions, and our reactions. True beauty represents what good we are offering to the world and can be evidenced in how we relate to and treat others, as well as how we relate to and treat ourselves. Our true beauty is reflected in how we perceive life, the world, and all of its perfections, and imperfections. It does not matter what we look at, what matters is how we are looking at it!

To most people beauty represents how we dress, how we look, how our body looks, the color of our skin, and what we've accomplished in life. But true beauty differs from those representations. There is a well-known saying that states "beauty is in the eye of the beholder." By terms of the dictionary, that statement intends to convey that if beauty is in the eye of the beholder, then the person who is observing gets to decide what is beautiful. By way of the dictionary, it also means that beauty cannot exist on its own, but is created by it observers. I both agree and disagree with those definitions. Beauty "as we know it" is created by its observers; but true beauty is created by God! And rather we choose to see the beauty or not in God's creations, it is still there! We don't get to observe and decide what God calls and made beautiful. **It just is!**

True beauty is that authentic quality within ourselves that makes us pleasant to be around. It is the humbleness, softness, gentleness, yet boldness of our being that keeps us real and relatable to ourselves, to God, and to other people. It is represented in our giving, our sharing, and all we are offering to the betterment of this world. Experiencing things or people in its authentic nature is beautiful! Some earthly 'true beauty" experiences are: watching the sunset, listening to birds sing, or watching a flower blossom into its fullest image. Another is watching the ocean or listening to the sound of the ocean. These are all genuine to their nature. They are all authentic and they are all destined and purposed to be and do exactly what it is they are being and doing.

A person walking in his or her authentic nature exemplifies true beauty. They are not beautiful because of what they physically look like, but they're beautiful because their heart, inner being, actions or work displays exactly what God created him or her to be. They are beautiful because they make us feel something different. We recognize something special about them. And we behold something genuine and life changing when we are in their presence!

Have you ever been in awe of anyone? Have you ever been in awe of anyone's gift or talent? Have you ever felt inspired, enlightened, or had goose bumps from either being in someone's presence or by watching and listening to them speak or perform in some manner? Have you ever felt chills or been overjoyed because of another's work, accomplishments, or skills? If you answered yes to any of those questions, that person has given you a "true beauty" experience.

There is true beauty in everyone. Along with our flaws, handicaps, and imperfections, there still lies true beauty within all of us that takes more than the mere human eye to see. True beauty has to be seen with the eyes of the heart and with the soul. We have the power to purposely make an effort to look for and acknowledge true beauty in all that God has created and placed into the world. It's ok to put effort into being beautiful on the outside, but become beautiful where it's going to count and matter the most to God. In a world where we can be whatever we want to be and can be as beautiful on the outside as we would like to be, let's also make an effort to become beautiful in the heart, in the mind, and in the soul. Recognize and acknowledge true beauty.

Treasure (3)

The Act of Pardoning

Pardon- to free from further punishment;
to forgive

Pardoning others and ourselves for things we have had to endure, process, and overcome in life can be extremely difficult. We are all familiar with the word forgiveness and we all understand why it is best to forgive. It is also important to know that whatever lies at the core of our hearts as it relates to the act of forgiveness will definitely determine the outcome (destruction or success) of situations in our lives. Forgiveness has the power to carry a whole lot of disaster (through unforgiveness), or a whole lot of destiny (through being able to forgive).

When we desire to move forward with forgiveness, we have to release both realistic and unrealistic expectations we have of ourselves, of others, and of life. No one is perfect and we must forgive ourselves and accept that we and others will make mistakes. We must accept that we won't always be able to make things happen like we want them to happen, and accept that things won't always be the way we think they should be.

Sometimes the process of forgiveness will attempt to play tricks on us. For example, we may get to places in our lives knowing we have taken the necessary steps to forgive others and ourselves, only to realize that forgiveness may not be a one-time declaration for us mere humans. In moving from one place of our lives into the next, we sometimes have to continuously make conscious decisions to continue forgiving others and ourselves for the same hurts and offenses we've already forgiven. That's because although we forgave the situation, parts of it may keep creeping back into our hearts and thoughts. That's ok and I've learned it's quite normal for that to happen. Let's not be tricked into thinking we haven't truly forgiven the person or situation. Instead, we must conquer the negative thoughts that continue to creep up. We conquer them by staying positive and continuing to walk in forgiveness. The more we stay positive and continue to walk in forgiveness, the less power we give to those type thoughts.

Unforgiveness definitely limits how much we are able to thrive and how far we are able to propel forward in life. Being able to forgive puts us on a path of higher consciousness mentally, emotionally, and spiritually. Over a period of time, that higher consciousness has the power to almost completely detach us from hurt and pain associated with past situations in our lives. If we are sincere about the process of growing, maturing, and becoming a better person, here are some exercises we can practice daily to utilize forgiveness and make our journey a bit smoother:

- When guilt, a bad thought, or a bad memory comes to mind or out of the mouth of others;

let's forgive others, ourselves, and move forward.

- When bad consequences are relentlessly beating down the doors of our lives, lets forgive others, ourselves, and move forward.
- When someone wants to sarcastically or negatively remind us of where we have been and all we have done wrong in life, let's forgive others, ourselves, and move forward.
- When temptations are put in our path to distract us, hold us back, or remind us of the road we once traveled, let's forgive others, ourselves, and move forward.

While on our journey to become a better person, temptations, past mistakes, bad habits, and the hurt and pain associated with situations we've experienced throughout life, will all be relentless in their efforts to tag along with us. They tag along as unproductive reminders, fears, insecurities, hardships, anger, depression, and all things that would like to keep us suppressed and despondent in life. We can deaden all that negativity as we stay positive and continue to productively move forward. We must move forward into the truth of what it takes to excel in life. Move forward into the truth of the person we are now. And move forward into the knowledge and understanding of the better person we desire to become. Activate forgiveness and keep it activated.

Treasure (4)

Love

Love is a gift from God that we've been supremely blessed to be given. 1 Peter 4:8-9 (NIV) tells us *"Above all, love each other deeply, because love covers a multitude of sin."* It also tells us to *"Offer hospitality to one another without grumbling."* Love is described as an intense feeling of deep affection and a feeling of warm personal attachment. Love brings about warmth, tenderness, intimacy, endearment, adoration, passion, praise, desire, and so many other wonderful things. I pray that everyone gets to experience what real love feels like and looks like. There are a lot of actions and situations in the world that people are calling love but are really not love.

Love wants what is best for people ... FOR ALL PEOPLE! Love is sincere. Love is caring and sharing. Love is respect. Love wants us to genuinely feel good about ourselves. Love wants us to prosper in life. Love wants us to be united and in harmony with one another. Love wants to uplift, support, and protect. Love wants to make us smile and make us laugh. Love gives us stability and security. Love wants us to grow and mature into our better selves. I'm not going to get into what I think love is NOT because I'm focusing on the positives. We should all be able to look at our lives based on the attributes I have just described love to be and decide if we are experiencing love or something else.

When becoming better people, we must be willing to invite and experience more love in our lives because God "IS" Love! If we want to be a part of Him and what He represents, we must release our hearts to receive and give love. Romans 13:8 (NIV) tell us to "*Let no debt remain outstanding, except the continuing debt to love one another, for WHOEVER LOVES OTHERS HAS FULFILLED THE LAW.*" And what is the law?

In Matthew 22: 35-40 (NIV), when the Pharisees got together and one of them (a law expert) tested Jesus and asked Him "which is the greatest commandment in the Law?" Jesus replied saying "we should love the Lord our God with all our heart, all our soul, and with all our minds." He said that was our first commandment; and our second commandment is "to love our neighbors as ourselves." And who are our neighbors? Allow me to answer this question in the spiritual sense. From reading Jesus's examples in Luke 10: 30-37 (NIV, and please read the scriptures for yourself), I would determine and conclude that our neighbors are any persons we can help and show genuine mercy and compassion to, as well as want justice for regardless of race, gender, color, and religion. In other words, God's love is meant to overcome and bring under subjection ALL prejudices! Let me repeat that! "GOD'S LOVE" IS MEANT TO OVERCOME AND BRING UNDER SUBJECTION "ALL PREJUDICES!" Godly Love should be at the base and center of ALL we do in life! If everyone exemplified that, this world would truly be grand after all. Now allow me to share with you a few earthly ways we can begin to invite and experience more love into our lives.

Accept Other's Differences

For the billions of people who exist in this world, we are all different! Not one of us is exactly the same. We all have our own separate set of fingerprints, footprints, DNA etc. We all represent different colors, different cultures, different sizes, different looks, and different everything. Again, not one of us is exactly the same as another. Because of that, there are going to be differences. The challenge here is learning to accept and embrace the difference of others (and sometimes ourselves) in a way that will allow us to love "anyhow."

We will experience many differences when it comes to ourselves and others. But the one thing all of us different people have in common is the fact that we are all human beings. It is the one common denominator that lies beneath all races, genders, personalities, characteristics, and physiques. Being a human being is the one link that connects us all on a level that goes far beyond looks, perceptions, prejudices, religions, and stereotypes. And as humans, we all have a God-given right to be acknowledged, accepted, and respected for being a fearfully and wonderfully made creation of God's magnificent handiwork (Psalm 139:14).

In keeping it real with myself, I personally might not like or may even intensely dislike the character or actions of some people, but I can love anybody. To love a person doesn't mean I have to live with them. To love a person doesn't mean I have to break bread with them. To love someone doesn't mean I have to be good friends with them or have dealings with them. Chavelle loving others simply means that I acknowledge and respect their presence and their existence (the fact that they are a human being and exist in this world), just as I am here existing. It means I acknowledge that we are all on a journey in this place we call life. It means I acknowledge that life is not easy for a whole lot of us, but we are all trying to figure it out as we navigate through it. It means, I acknowledge that everyone is a creation of God's and because I truly love Him, I can genuinely love all that He created.

Chavelle loving God's creations also means I will never do anything intentionally to hurt or harm anyone. It means I will never try to suppress, hold back, or keep anybody down. But know that I love me too! And if a person can't or won't give me the same level of respect that I am willing to give to them, and if they can't love me in a healthy and uplifting way, then I must put some distance between us because I won't be discredited or discounted! And I won't be denied or disrespected! I can love people just because they are a child of God's and just because I don't "have" to hate them. I don't have to be around them or in their space, but I can still love God's creations.

Now that is absolutely freeing to me! It's freeing because I choose to genuinely love, but with my truths! And genuinely loving with my truths comes without pressure or expectations. They also come without having to fit inside the status quo of how society tells me to love. I choose to have a sense of love for everybody because in my world, no matter how awful some people can be, they are just not worth "me" hating. Hating them is not worth all that negative energy to me! Again, I can hate how they act or their actions. I can hate how they think or something they might say, but I don't have to hate them. And I'm not going to hate them. But that's just me and how I "choose" to invite and experience more love into my life. I'm not attempting to speak for everybody on this matter.

We can love people without loving what they do or what they represent. We can even love people despite what situations, teachings, or unknown circumstances may have negatively taught a person to become. Loving a person in this sense doesn't mean to bow down or keep quiet in the face of injustices or wrong doings. Loving in this sense simply means to find a way to be heard, to be constructive, and to be able to move mountains in the face of the injustices in a proud and conventional way. God loves us in the midst of our sins and wrong doings and though it may be a very long stretch to say we can love others that way, I am here to tell you that it is humanly and Godly possible.

If we can possibly see ourselves as mothers, fathers, brothers, sisters, aunts, uncles, nieces, nephews, cousins and children to all, we can all sense a feeling of having love for everyone. Some people we will love with great and unconditional love, and some people we will love at the minimum and with boundaries in place. People love differently and that is ok. As long as we are using love to build each other up and not tear one another down, the degree to how much we love should not be the focus. We definitely won't be able to love everyone "greatly," but just because we can't, it doesn't give us the right to discount, disrespect, and disregard another human being. Love in this sense doesn't have to be perfect, but it should be tolerable, forgiving, and genuine.

Accepting peoples' differences is vital to our growth and maturity. Embracing this skill will be a blessed gem to have in our lives. We are all a part of one universe; all races and all genders are a part of this universe! We can love beyond racial and gender differences without loving or accepting discriminating actions and behaviors. And though it is not easy, we can also love through rejection, wrong-doing, and hate. All people and all things have a purpose and a place of order in life. It is when people and things are without purpose, out of place, and out of order, that fears, intimidations, misuse, abuse, as well as hate gets involved. This is one reason why we must be observant and aware of what is going on around us. We have to use common sense and have boundaries set in our lives for situations where hate is prevalent. Accepting other's differences does not mean to be naive and in the dark about very real situations, very real prejudices, and very real injustices that goes on in the world. Accept other's differences but be mindful of what you will and will not accept, tolerate, and allow in your life.

Note: Thank God we are all different people. That is a necessity because if people were all the same, life would be boring and no one would really be able to help, teach, inspire, influence, or learn from anyone right? There would not be a need for gifts, talents, role models, or others to look up to. None of that would really matter if we were all the same. Allow more love to enter into your hearts by accepting others differences. It will enlighten and enrich your path to becoming a better person.

Agree to Disagree

By no means do we all have to think alike or act alike. Yet, some of us are easily offended when others offer opinions that are totally different from the way we think. This is sad and disappointing to say, but differences of opinions have been the root and cause of a lot of violence, broken relationships, and deaths in this world. Not being able to agree to disagree keeps us from respecting others voices and moving forward as a whole. It causes friction and friction begets other disturbances.

Accepting that it's okay for you to have your opinion and for me to have my opinion will help us to stay civil in a sometimes uncivilized situation. What another person says or think does not have to take away from the things we choose to believe. It doesn't have to take away from the person we truly are or the person we are trying to become. Things people may say or think about us do not have the power to define us, alter our dreams, or affect the way we choose to live our lives unless we agree with it. When people are offering opinions that aren't productive or is not constructive criticism, their opinions will only have power over us if we surrender to what they say and react negatively because of it. Agreeing to disagree gives us the strength to stay calm. It allows us to respect people who think differently than us. It gives us the power to move forward in healthy and productive ways. Agree to disagree and be respectful of others.

Observe and Acknowledge Nature

Observing and acknowledging nature is a sure way to invite and experience more love into our lives. The study of nature can teach us so much about life and the simplicity of it. Observing nature helps us to understand patience and time. Nature enlightens us on the process of transformation and how a lot of things just naturally come into their own being with little or no help from anybody but God and His natural resources.

What God naturally brings to life in environments where there is no manipulation, no selfishness, no hidden agendas, no self-wills, and no ulterior motives is utterly amazing! The results of these type manifestations hold much power in its own right because in an environment like that, all things are genuinely free to become exactly what they are destined and purposed to be. They are not hindered by fears or insecurities, and will not stop or be deterred because of what others may think or say about who or what they are.

Nature by definition means all things in the universe. It is the physical world and everything in it that is not made by man. To acknowledge and have respect for nature in its most natural sense is to say that we are aware of the existence of a higher power. We are acknowledging that there is definitely something supernaturally extraordinary about the world we live in! Nature is evidence that evolution exists and it manifests a visible end result for every visible beginning. Nature shows us that everything happens in its own perfect timing and matures to the very best of its concept. Nature definitely shows us reproduction and as long as nature's reproductions are not being tampered with, whatever is being reproduced will always be true to its kind. For examples: animals will always reproduce animals of its kind, humans will always reproduce humans, apples will always reproduce apples, etc. All things WILL stay true to its kind unless someone interferes with its natural process in order to create something else. Something NOT of natural nature!

Being in a world filled with such advanced and masterminded technology, it is great to know we can still count on nature to reproduce from natural abilities. It's good to know that natural metamorphosis still play a significant role in our universe. Yes, as advanced and masterminded as science and technology is today, acknowledging and respecting the simplicity of nature does testify to the fact that God does and forever will exist! And how can we not feel and experience some type of love when we talk about God and witness all of His greatness and sovereignty, especially when it comes to nature!

Treasure (5)

Purpose

Purpose is the reason something or someone is created. It is the reason why people and things exist. Purpose is something a lot of us seek to know and fulfill in our lives. It gives us our life meaning and a clear direction as we move along in life. A person without purpose is almost like a wanderer in life. That means they kind of just live life day to day and move along as life comes to them. That's not to criticize anyone or to put anybody down because although I kind of knew my purpose, I was still like a wanderer trying to find my place inside of it.

Knowing there is greater meaning as to why we are born and not be able to grasp or fully connect with that meaning, well that can make a person feel lost or feel as if God forgot to gift them with purpose. But know that we all have purpose! Some people's purpose stands out and is immediately recognizable. We see it manifesting through their gifts, their works, and their talents. Other's purpose may be more subtle or unclear. When gifts and talents don't automatically stand out in our lives, seeking to fulfill and understanding purpose within ourselves can be long, challenging, and frustrating.

The best way to know our true purpose is to connect with The One who has the beginning and the ending of who we are and what we are to become in this world. It's the person who knows our greatest potentials and capabilities. It is the One who distributes the gifts, the talents, and purposed us in the first place (and no, He did not skip over you). That person is God! In Psalm 32:8 (NIV) God says: *"I will instruct you and teach you in the way you should go; I will counsel you with my loving eye.* Jeremiah 29:11 (NIV) reads: *"For I know the plans I have for you,"* declares the Lord, *"plans to prosper you and not to harm you, plans to give you hope and a future."* Ephesians 2:10 (NIV) reads: *"For we are God's handiwork, created in Christ Jesus to do good works, which God prepared in advance for us to do."* These scriptures prove that God created us with plans and purpose already in mind.

In my humbled opinion, I don't feel our purpose is something we find or stumble into. I feel that way because purpose is a lot deeper than that. People who are truly living in their purpose will tell you it was something they were already doing or something they have felt about themselves all along. They will tell you it is something that seemed to have come to them very naturally although they did not fully recognize it, understand it, or knew how to put it into proper perspective. They will tell you their purpose was always a part of them even when they weren't aware at the time that it was actually purpose!

Purposeful (purpose driven) people truly believe they were born to do something relevant and to be someone who generates light and a sense of togetherness in the world. They feel missioned to bring healing and unity into the world in one way or another. They give of themselves in ways that will help to make life easier and better for others. Living out God's purpose allows us to give a small piece of His heart and a small feel of His touch to the world. People get to know and become aware of who God is because of other people functioning in their purpose.

Now catch this - purposeful people believe they were born to do what they do, but because purpose is deeper than our gifts and our talents, it is for the mere sake of purpose we have the gifts and talents in the first place. For example: a singer might say he or she was born to sing, but the purpose is not actually in the gift or talent of singing. That's just the avenue it is expressed through. Purpose validates a need for the creation and it fulfills the need for life changing aspirations like breaths of life, healing, hope, and answers for the soul. Because of that, purpose goes a lot deeper than the gift or talent and results in a singer being able to have a healing, soothing, joyous, and harmonious effect on people through their emotions, (thoughts, feelings) and actions while listening to a singer's songs. Another example: a doctor might say he or she was born to be a doctor, but their purpose is not in being a doctor and giving diagnosis or writing prescriptions. Their purpose is in their ability to help heal peoples' physical, emotional, or mental ailments. There is a difference between talents, gifts, works, and purpose.

Now tell me this, if the expression of life (life itself) was summoned to take notice of you by following you around and writing your story, what would life say about you? In what form would the expression of life even know that you exist in this world? What is your heart and soul unselfishly saying and expressing loud enough that it makes the goodness of life take notice, pay you some real attention, and make room for you? Take some time to think about that question.

God's purpose in our lives says to the world, "if God could not directly speak to you, you can still hear a little of God's voice through my _____ (whatever we are authentically offering to the betterment of humanity and the world)." God's purpose in our lives says to the world, "if God could not physically touch you, you can still feel a little of God's love and God's touch through my _____ (whatever we are authentically offering to the betterment of humanity and the world)." God's purpose in our lives says to the world' "though you cannot see God, you can see the hand of God moving through my _____ (whatever we are authentically offering to the betterment of humanity and the world)." A person functioning in their purpose will be able to complete one or all of those statements above. Purpose comes directly from the heart and soul. It is a direct, intentional, meaningful, and authentic inner giving of ourselves that is expressed outwardly through many different works, gifts, talents, and avenues.

When we are becoming better people, we are apt to start looking for meaning in our lives and desiring to want to know our purpose. It is a part of what satisfies the hunger and yearning of belonging and total acceptance in our hearts. As our purpose begins to unfold in our lives, it puts us on a path to becoming authentic and true to what we feel we are created for. And once we know why we are created, we desire to contribute that missing piece to the world. We desire to be useful to the cause of our being. Knowing and living out our purpose is our way of boldly saying and proclaiming to the world, "I AM MEANT TO BE HERE!" Whether it is on a small stage or a big stage, whether it is in our community or across the world, whether it is on our jobs, in our churches, or in our homes, purpose pulls us up front and makes life take notice that we exist and are ready to stand in the truth of who we are.

Note: No, I don't feel we find or stumble into purpose. We may find and stumble into opportunities. We may find and stumble into passions. We may even stumble into our gifts and talents. But purpose, that is something that has been with us from the very beginning of our existence. Yes, from the very first second we entered into this world, we arrived with purpose. In possibly subtle or maybe even indirect ways, our purpose has always been a part of our lives. God defines our purpose and He has each person's definition of who they are waiting for all the ones who dare to seek Him for it. Where there is purpose, there is power! Where there is purpose, there is God's validation!

Treasure (6)

Prayer

Then Jesus told His disciples a parable to show them that they should always pray and not give up. Luke 18:1 (NIV)

What is prayer? Prayer is our conversation with God. It is a two-way dialogue between Him and us individually or as a group. Prayer serves as a channel that keeps us tuned in to our Creator. It surrenders us to the authority and mercies of God. What make prayer powerful is the consistency and the authenticity of it and our hearts. Prayer is powerful when it is filled with God's word, order, love, compassion, warmth, and selflessness. Meditation engages our thoughts, our thinking, and our reflecting while prayer communicates it to God. Prayer and meditation is a way to keep our sanity in a world filled with much insanity (hurt, hate, disappointments, and dysfunction). It is a way to keep us humbled and submitted to a higher power - The Higher Power (God)!

Prayer and meditation are necessary treasures to have on our path to becoming a better person. They both are peaceful and calming acts which gives us an open and non-condemning platform before God. During prayer, we can be as real and as transparent as we want to be with God. A life filled with prayer and meditation continuously invites God into our daily living. And there is nothing compared to having someone so loving, so gentle, so comforting, so peaceful, so merciful, so forgiving, so compassionate - I could go on and on about the wonderful characteristics of God. But trust me when I say that there is nothing like having someone like Him to share our hearts and the many challenges of ups and downs we experience in our lives with.

Daily conversations with God through prayer and meditation are so refreshing. God never reminds us of our mistakes, flaws, or anything about our yesterdays, unless He is revealing it for a greater good in our lives. He never holds reminders over our heads to punish us or to use them against us. Instead, He forgives us our trespasses and allows us to move on. Our conversation with Him allows Him to speak directly to our hearts to guide us, to love on us, and to heal us. Ephesians 6:18 says, we ought to always pray. (NIV) *And pray in the Spirit on all occasions with all kinds of prayer and requests. With this in mind, be alert and always keep on praying for all of the Lord's people.* Prayer gives us strength and clarity in life. With God, prayer really does change things!

Note: If you allow yourself to fully embrace these six treasures I have shared with you, you will open yourself up to receive more of the goodness of what life has to offer. God has a new way of life with our names written on it. But it is up to us to get to this desired place.

10. Making a Difference

There is absolute joy in having the resources and the willingness to make a difference in someone's life and in to the world. It is a blessing to partake of fulfilling some type of spiritual, physical, emotional, or financial need in the lives of others. Nothing brings more of a heart-warming sense of satisfaction and purpose being fulfilled than knowing we have used resources like our gifts, our talents, our experiences, our works, our money, and every good thing we have to offer to the world in order to encourage, inspire, influence, and be of some help to others. There are great rewards in helping to meet the needs of another in a selfless, loving, and compassionate way. Nothing compares to knowing we have done something beneficial and positive, great or small, to better humanity!

What a blessing to be able to live life to our fullest potential, while being a source that can help to make a difference in the lives of others. No act of caring or kindness is insignificant or too small when it comes to helping others. Making an earnest difference in this world is one way of knowing that our living will not be in vain. We come into this world through birth; and we will leave this world through death. And what will matter after those two very major and life changing events is what we have done in-between them.

One of my very best friends died at an early age. She was around 30 years old when God decided to call her home to Him. As I sat at her funeral, I could not help but think thoughts like, did she say all she wanted to say to her kids, to her Mom, and to her family? I wondered did she secretly want to do some things but never had the courage to do them. Months after the death of my friend, I spoke to her Mom. It gave me great joy to hear her Mom say that my friend was in such a beautiful and peaceful place when she transitioned from this life into God's arms. I knew then that whether she said all she wanted to say, or did all she wanted to do ... was something she and God had made peace about. But did she have time to make a difference in the life of someone else? Yes, very much so! Especially in the life of her devoted and loving mother who, day after day and night after night, nurtured her, listened to her, loved her, comforted her, prayed for her, and became a great source of God's strength that her beautiful daughter could totally trust and depend on.

The precious moments between my friend and her Mom gave her Mom the love and the strength she needed to raise her daughter's young children (her grandchildren). It also gave her Mom the strength to smile despite her great loss. Most importantly, those precious moments with her daughter gave her Mom the love and strength she needed to move forward when she wanted so much to live in those last moments and last conversations with her daughter. Those moments gave her great peace during the times she desired to have her daughter, and her grandchildren's mother, there in the home with them. My friend made the difference that gave her Mother absolutely everything she needed to make a beautiful difference in the lives of her grandchildren and so many other people.

Again, it is a blessing to be given the opportunity to make a difference in the life of someone else. At any given moment, we can take our last breath upon this earth. When that moment comes, what is it that will really matter to us in the few seconds that precedes us departing this life? Remember, when making a difference in the lives of others, the blessing is not in how great or small our contribution to humanity is. The blessing is in our willingness to give, to share, and to equally and earnestly want the same good for others, that we want or have for ourselves, for our very own children, for our parents, and for all the people who are dear to us. The blessing is in seeing a need and doing our part to fill that need or to help in some considerate way.

When we don't have resources available to meet the needs of another, sometimes our part may only be to pray and intercede on their behalf. But if a cup of water is all we have to offer to someone who is thirsty, by all means, we can do our part by offering that cup of water. If a morsel of food is all we have available to offer to someone who is hungry, by all means, we can do our part and offer that morsel of food. If a free ride to the doctor or the grocery store is all we can offer to someone who doesn't have a vehicle, by all means, we can do our part by offering that free ride.

God honors the little we earnestly give out of love, mercy and compassion a lot quicker than He will honor someone who gives a lot only to be praised and recognized for it. This is what Mark 12: 41-44 (NIV) has to say about that. *Jesus sat down opposite the place where the offerings were put and watched the crowd putting their money into the temple treasury. Many rich people threw in large amounts. But a poor widow came and put in two very small copper coins worth only a few cents. Calling his disciples to him, Jesus said, "Truly I tell you, this poor widow has put more into the treasury than all the others. They all gave out of their wealth; but she, OUT OF HER POVERTY, PUT IN EVERYTHING - ALL SHE HAD TO LIVE ON."*

The poor widow only put a few cents (2 very small copper coins) into the offering but God honored her two copper coins because it was ALL SHE HAD! Jesus saw more than the poor widow's two copper coins. He saw her heart. We should never let our reasoning for wanting to make a difference in the lives of others be vain or be prideful! Making a difference should come from a genuine and compassionate place. And it definitely should come from a place of love. I am sure God cares more about how and why we touch the lives of others, rather than how many lives we touch. I believe even if we only made a convicted difference in the life of one person, please know that one person could go on to make a difference in the lives of hundreds, thousands, or millions. Our heartfelt contribution to that one person is just as important as he or she being able to make a difference in the lives of many others. When we use all we have (figuratively speaking and with discernment) to be a blessing to someone (anyone), God will honor that!

Note: Making a difference is such a selfless act. God does not ask or expect us to save the entire world, but if we do our part with the love, compassion, and resources He has given and provides for us, we can all find a way to contribute to the betterment of mankind. It is an opportunity we all can partake in. Make a difference and you will help change the world!

11. In Conclusion

This conclusion gave me so much joy to write. It gave me joy because I was excited to explain how it took so many paths and so many stops along my journey of becoming a better me to really get to know myself and come into the person I am today. On my many paths, I would accomplish something then say "ok, this is where I'm supposed to be in life; this is what I'm supposed to be doing, and this place right here is where I belong!" I would get all excited about where I was in life only to have circumstances and consequences come around and dismantle my place. I can't tell you how many times I've started a new venture in life! And what's really surreal is how all of my starting anew has brought me back to a place I dreamed about years ago as a teenager. That's a place of being an inspirational/motivational teacher and a writer of inspirational self-help books.

I look back now and know this was my calling (my avenue of purpose), from the very beginning. As a child and teenager, I always had an indescribable compassion for others. I was always a deep thinker and intrigued by wanting to know what made people feel like they felt, did what they did, or why they acted a certain way. At an early age in life, I took on burdens of other people as if it was my responsibility to help them feel better or help them figure things out. I couldn't say why I started doing things like that at such a young age; I was just "so to speak" wired that way.

I remember I bought my 1st self-help book around the age of 16. I didn't think anything was wrong with me or anybody I knew; I was just drawn to those type books, certain types of people, and anything with some sort of psychology or counselor feel to it. I didn't think I wanted to be a psychologist or counselor. At that time, and being the country girl I am, I didn't even know what a psychologist or a counselor was. I just knew I had a deep uncontrollable passion for the mindset, for behaviors, for people, and how it all worked together. I didn't think what I was intrigued about was something I should explore or pursue in life as a career choice.

After purchasing my first self-help book at age 16, I eventually became the proud owner of many self-help books. I read a lot of different book, but some I connected with on such an incredible level that I can only describe the experience as being a genuine comfort to my heart, mind, and my spirit. In other words, everything just felt right! A lot of the thoughts and insight in the self-help books were very parallel to my own thoughts and insight on a lot of issues. So to find kindred spirits in authors who looked at the world in a lot of the same ways I saw the world was refreshing and life altering to me. Some of the self-help books made me feel like my abnormal "very mature" way of thinking at such an early age was actually normal. I felt a sense of belonging! I felt a sense of belonging but I didn't understand all that. I still had to find my way in life because everything (the gifts, the talents, the passion, the very mature thinking, the curiosity, and the purpose) still wasn't clear to me. And honestly, at such a young age, I wasn't really trying to dig deep into anything on those particular matters. I was young, living life, and just liked what I liked. But once I was in my mid-twenties, I started trying to make sense of all the things in my life. That became the beginning of me being in pursuit of the life I was subconsciously trying to understand and search for. Now let me tell you what my reality was.

Because I had no real idea of who I was as a person, (just inklings or pieces of life I could not fully comprehend or fit together), nor did I know anything about passion or purpose, I went on to pursue a career in fashion design and cosmetology after high school. I knew I was a free spirit kind of person and possibly could not work a 9 to 5 job; therefore, I catered more to the arts. I knew I was creative. I loved drawing. And I figured as a fashion designer and cosmetologist, I could help people look good and feel good about themselves. Fashion design school got very expensive so I dropped out and focused more on cosmetology. I received my license to style hair and set out on my journey. It was great! I set my own hours and I was able to work along beside friends I could laugh and joke with all day. I was pleased in this field of work and I was blessed with the opportunity to meet many wonderful people and make great lifetime friends. No two days were the same and I absolutely loved that! The best part of it all was that I was able to do what I mostly had a passion for in the first place. That was listening to my customers and subconsciously, yet naturally, offering insight and inspiration when I could.

Though cosmetology was a very good and fulfilling career, it didn't fulfill my soul. So while in my cosmetology profession, I found myself dabbling in other business ventures trying to find the answer to what my soul was yearning for. I did everything from selling Mary Kay products to opening a specialty wig boutique for people who were dealing with hair loss. In everything I did, I thought, ok, this is it! I'm helping people, I feel like I'm making a difference, this is definitely the place I'm supposed to be. Yet, none of those businesses felt satisfying or authentic to what I truly felt in my heart. Though they were all good and helpful occupations, nothing felt exactly right and none of them stopped the yearning in my soul.

I don't feel as if anything I did was in vain, nor do I regret any of the other business ventures (besides the money spent). I actually believe I needed all those different paths; and after 25 plus years of being a cosmetologist, life also brought me to a place where I had to semi-retire from that profession. Semi-retiring left me with a very uncomfortable feeling of discomfort and displacement. It put me a position to have to wrestle and struggle with life and with God. But now I know, those moments were all divinely purposed to lead me back to the place where I started years before as a child/teenager. That was down the path of becoming the person I am today.

Life finally presented me the opportunity to become the person I felt in my heart I would be years ago. I began to see how life had strategically given me all the tools I needed to become an inspirational/motivational teacher and a writer of inspirational self-help books. Life began answering all the questions as to why I thought the way I did as a child, why I always took on the burdens of other people, and why I've always been intrigued with psychology and self-help books. Those were all inklings of who I was to become; only I wasn't equipped or experienced enough to fully understand or handle such a task of how to truly help myself and others back then.

Isn't that amazing? Isn't God amazing! It took many turn arounds, many lessons learned, many paths, and many wrong stops in my life to bring me to this place of fulfillment. But here I am, and I'm on schedule as it relates to God's perfect timing. I'm saying all of that to say to you, life is definitely a journey and our journey may be filled with all types of trials and tribulations. But God uses all we have experienced in life for the glorifying of His kingdom and to get us where we need to be "when" we need to be there! I needed all those paths and the many experiences to be the person I am today. They were all strategically designed to give me a testimony and make me a better person.

As I come to the end of writing this book, I am truly humbled as to how I've reached another milestone on my journey of becoming a better me. I am living a life with meaning and with not only purpose, but with God's purpose for me. I am by no means a perfect person, nor do I have all the answers to life. But with the help of God, I am in a place where I can offer the wisdom and experience I have to help others in a caring, healthy, and sincere way. I have overcome a lot of life's challenges and have navigated my way through a lot of life's potholes to get here! Right now, I'm dwelling in a place of hope, healing, peace, and genuine happiness.

The overall experience of writing this book entailed a lot of ups and downs. It entailed a lot of getting it right and settled with myself "first" because I dare not present to you or place before you or anyone, a plate that I have not eaten from or a road I have never traveled. I dare not present before you something I have never lived, never experienced, nor never applied to my own life. I honestly and earnestly desire to be who I say I am and to do what I ask of others to do.

Through everything I have experienced in life thus far, my journey has taught me that our journeys are forever changeable and ongoing. I've learned that it's ok to live life happy, a little free-hearted, and to totally trust God with our lives. For God knows the plans He has for us. God really does care and He wants us to have the desires of our hearts. However, we can't be afraid to venture out, and we can't be afraid to try. We can't be afraid to get it wrong or fail, and we can't be afraid to go in another direction. This is called life and it is called growth. And through all of our faults, our failures, our flaws, our shortcomings, and all of our successes, I, Chavelle Dallas, and you - can continuously become "A Better Me." Cheers to your journey of becoming A Better You! You can do this! Much Love and Strength to you!

Note: Since traveling upon this new journey, I have come across a community of kindred spirits. I am thankful to God for allowing me to be in the presence of such amazing and inspiring people. When you find your true path in life, life begins to synchronize itself. Coincidences no longer exist. Everything comes into play by divine order and is there to help us in some way along our journey!

"I may not always be at my best, but I thank God I now have the maturity, the wisdom, the power, and the strength, to not allow life's situations or people, to have me at my worst!"

-Chavelle Dallas-

** My life was like a colorful Rubik's Cube ... filled with the chaos of many different colors representing many different stages in my life. Then one day ... all the colors of my life lined up in synchronized order! I discovered my place in this world and my life changed FOREVER!**
**#IAMABETTERME! **

-*Chavelle Dallas*-

To send comments or have Chavelle Dallas host

"A Better Me" Workshop at your church, at an event,

or in your area:

Please contact her by visiting her website

chavelledallas.com

email: contact@chavelledallas.com

Also available for Book Signings & Author visits

Please subscribe to Chavelle's YouTube Channel:

Chavelle Dallas/Monday Massages with Chavelle

"YouTube Channel Coming Soon"

Follow her on:

Instagram: Chavelle Dallas Inspirations

And like her Facebook page:

Chavelle Dallas Inspirations

~~~~~~~~~~~~~~~~~~~~~~~~

cd Inspirations/Chavelle Dallas

P.O. Box 16433

Fernandina Beach, Florida 32035

References

Kreitzen, Mary Jo. "Why Relationships are Important." *Taking Charge of your Health and Wellbeing*, n.p.

Retrieved September 2017 from:

https://www.takingcharge.csh.umn.edu/why-personal-relationships-are-important

"Families and Relationships" Retrieved (2017) from

https://www.apa.org/helpcenter/family/index.aspx

www.ingramcontent.com/pod-product-compliance
Lightning Source LLC
LaVergne TN
LVHW011208080426
835508LV00007B/659